Interpretationshilfen

Macbeth

William Shakespeare

Cornelsen

Alan Pulverness
Macbeth · Interpretationshilfe

Verlagsredaktion
Neil Porter

Umschlagdesign
Klein & Halm Grafikdesign, Berlin

Layout & technische Umsetzung
Anna Bakalović und Annika Preyhs, Berlin

Picture credits: p. 5: © akg-images; p. 7: the Bridgeman Art Library/private collection; p. 9: the Bridgeman Art Library/Walker Art Gallery, National Museums, Liverpool; p. 10: the Bridgeman Art Library; p. 15: the Bridgeman Art Library/private collection; p. 16: the Bridgeman Art Library/British Library, London, UK; p. 42: CINETEXT; p. 49: CINETEXT/Sammlung Beyl

www.cornelsen.de

1. Auflage, 1. Druck 2006

Druck: CS-Druck CornelsenStürtz, Berlin

ISBN-13: 978-3-589-22223-0
ISBN-10: 3-589-22223-9

Inhalt gedruckt auf säurefreiem Papier aus nachhaltiger Forstwirtschaft.

Contents

All page and line references are to the Cornelsen edition of *Macbeth* (Berlin: Cornelsen Verlag, 2005) ISBN 978-3-589-22223-0.

William Shakespeare (1564–1616)

Surprisingly little is known about William Shakespeare, considering he that is probably the most famous playwright who ever lived.

He was born in Stratford-upon-Avon in April 1564. He married Anne Hathaway in 1582, with whom he had three children, Susanna, Hamnet and Judith. Little else is known about him until 1592, when Shakespeare is mentioned as being a playwright. It is also known that he worked as an actor and that he was part-owner of a playing company (a company of actors) called 'The Lord Chamberlain's Men'. In 1603 King James took over the patronage of the company and it was renamed 'The King's Men'. Shakespeare became a wealthy man and bought properties in London and Stratford. He retired to Stratford in around 1614 and died there on 23 April 1616.

During his lifetime he wrote 37 plays. He may have written more but these have not survived. Although 18 of his plays were published during his lifetime, most of these editions (called 'quartos') were probably not overseen by Shakespeare. Their texts may have been reconstructed from memory by a member or members of the cast of the plays.

It was only in 1623 that his plays were first published in what is called 'The Folio'. But as Shakespeare was by then dead, it cannot be said that the Folio is a definitive text. However, it was the first time that many of his plays, including *Macbeth*, were printed.

Shakespeare is unusual in that he wrote a wide variety of plays. Not only did he write history plays that covered over a hundred years of English history, he was also equally competent at tragedy (e.g. *Hamlet*) as well as comedy (e.g. *Much Ado about Nothing*).

Besides being a playwright, he was also a prolific poet: he wrote a cycle of 154 sonnets as well as several long poems.

Shakespeare's reputation grew slowly after his death, but by the end of the 20th century he had become the most performed dramatist in the world. Many of the lines from his plays and poems are still well-known today.

Historical Background

Political Stability and Chaos

The world in which Shakespeare wrote *Macbeth* (ca. 1606) was one in which peaceful rule could all too easily be disrupted. England's recent past had been turbulent, but the country had remained relatively stable despite the many threats to it. Here are some key events and problems that had faced England over the previous 200 years:

The War of the Roses (1455–1485): This civil war between rival families over their claims to the English throne had devastated England. It only ended when the Tudors defeated Richard III in battle. There was a constant fear that civil war might break out again (as in fact it did in 1642). Shakespeare knew this particular period of English history very well, and his 'history plays' cover the period. The plays are *Henry IV (Parts I and II)*, *Henry V*, *Henry VI (Parts I, II and III)* and *Richard III*.

The religious conflict: The Reformation had reached England early, and the country had changed its religious practices more than once during the reign of the Tudors. By 1600 there was a large Catholic minority, while a Protestant movement called Puritanism was trying to influence the Church of England, which was itself trying to steer a middle course between Protestantism and Catholicism. Much of

The Gunpowder Plot conspirators (Guy Fawkes is third from right)

continental Europe was a battlefield in the religious wars between Catholics and Protestants, and many in England feared that their country, too, might get involved. There were many Catholic plots against Elizabeth and James, including the most famous, the Gunpowder Plot of 1605 led by Guy Fawkes, which had intended to blow up Parliament. Shakespeare may even have known some of the conspirators; several of them came from near Stratford and drank at Shakespeare's favourite inn, the Mermaid Tavern.

The fear of foreign invasion: Many Catholics looked to Spain to end their oppression. Until the defeat of the Spanish Armada in 1588 (when Shakespeare was 23), there was a very real fear in England of a foreign invasion. Although there was no longer the threat of a Spanish invasion, the English had developed a very strong fear of Spain and other Catholic countries.

The political revolts: In the period leading up to the death of the childless Queen Elizabeth, there was growing political discontent. In 1601 the Queen's favourite, the Earl of Essex, together with a band of men, tried to force his presence on the Queen. He was declared a traitor and executed. This revolt was a symptom of political uncertainty, as the succession to the English throne was not clear, and it was only a matter of time before Queen Elizabeth would die. Shakespeare had been marginally involved in this revolt, since his friend and patron, the Earl of Southampton, had been one of the conspirators imprisoned by the Queen. Moreover, Essex had paid to have Shakespeare's play *Richard II* performed at the Globe Theatre on the eve of his revolt. Queen Elizabeth was outraged when she learned of this, allegedly saying 'I am Richard II, know you not?' *Richard II* may have been intended as a political comment on the contemporary situation, with the weak Richard II being seen as Queen Elizabeth. The play could be seen as arguing in favour of her replacement by a monarch capable of creating a stable dynasty.

The dynastic succession: Nowadays people look back to the reign of Queen Elizabeth as England's Golden Age, but in the last years of her reign, the ageing queen had lost some of her popularity. It was uncertain who would succeed her. According to the will of Henry VIII, the Tudors should be succeeded by the descendants of his younger sister. However, the main claimant, Lady Anne Stanley, was unmarried and not very charismatic. For the last years of Elizabeth's reign, it was presumed that the descendant of Henry VIII's elder sister, King James VI of Scotland, would become the next monarch of England. Indeed, this turned out to be the case, but the union of England and Scotland under a Scottish king was seen more as the best option rather than as a popular move. In the event, the succession occurred smoothly and peacefully.

Queen Elizabeth I

So Shakespeare and his contemporaries were well aware of how easily the country's peace could be shattered and how political chaos was never far away. Indeed, many of Shakespeare's plays demonstrate the fear of political disruption and a return to the anarchy of civil war. The theme of the loss of order runs through the nine history plays, written during the 1590s, that cover the period of England's political unrest during the War of the Roses. It is also shown in the chaos that follows the killing of Julius Caesar in Shakespeare's play of the same name, and becomes one of the central themes of *Macbeth*.

Crucial to political stability at the time was the strength of the monarch. As all important political decisions were made by the monarch, it was essential that he or she played a strong but just role in English life. Since 1603 the new monarch had been King James I, who had been King James VI of Scotland since 1567.

King James

King of Scotland

King James

James was born in 1566 and was just a child when his Catholic mother, Mary, Queen of Scots, was forced to leave Scotland in 1567. So at a very young age, he became James VI of Scotland. James was brought up in Scotland as a member of the Presbyterian Church of Scotland, adhering to a religion in which equality played an important part. Unlike other national churches where ritual and the anointing of the monarch played an important role, the link between God and King was not emphasized in the Presbyterian Church. Insecure in a country in which lords and religious leaders had little regard for the monarch (his own mother had been deposed), James was much more sensitive to the role of the king in society and reacted by being among the first to develop the idea of the '**divine right of kings**'. He wrote *The True Law of Free Monarchies* in 1598 and circulated it anonymously, before publishing it in 1603. Another publication written by James is the *Basilikon Doron* (1599). It was intended as a guide for the conduct of his son Henry when he became king (Henry, however, died young). In it James warned Henry of ministers who interfere too much and explained again the doctrine of the divine right of kings. This doctrine reflected his absolutist attitudes. Moreover, in a speech before Parliament he once said: 'The state of monarchy is the supremest thing upon earth; for kings are not only God's lieutenants upon earth, and sit upon God's throne, but even by God himself are called gods.'

Indeed, one might think that James felt more comfortable in England than in Scotland, where deference to the monarchy was more widespread, if not universal.

Furthermore, James believed that he himself had certain divine powers, amongst them the practice of touching people suffering from the disease scrofula, known as 'the Evil'. Shakespeare portrays King Edward the Confessor of England performing the same act (IV, iii, 141–158) – precisely at the point in the play when Malcolm and Macduff are deliberating how they can rid themselves of Macbeth, thereby highlighting the difference between the two monarchs, the good and the tyrannical.

However, despite his belief in his own divine power, James suffered from revolts and power struggles in Scotland. Perhaps the most serious in his later years was his attempted kidnapping by the Earl of Gowrie. In 1600, three years before he became King James I of England, James was attacked by the Earl of Gowrie while he was staying in Gowrie's house. In his attempt to murder the King, Gowrie (much like Macbeth) had broken the ancient laws of loyalty and hospitality. The Gowrie conspiracy undoubtedly had a major effect on James. This conspiracy caused much tension in Scotland and was followed closely in England, as James was seen to be Elizabeth's likely successor.

The Union of Two Nations

Perhaps one of the most remarkable events to take place in British history was the accession of the Scottish king to the English throne, as the union of the Scottish and English crowns was anything but inevitable. The Tudor dynasty was one of the most colourful to have ruled England, and under Queen Elizabeth, England's future course as an imperial power had been set. However, the Tudors found it notoriously difficult to produce heirs; Henry VIII's policies were often determined by the need to have a male heir, and in the end none of his three children (Edward VI, Mary I and Elizabeth I) managed to have children. Henry VIII had feared that the English crown would go to a Scot: in his will, he excluded his sister, Margaret Tudor (who had married King James IV of Scotland and was therefore James VI's grandmother) and her descendants from the line of succession. However, following the execution of his mother, Mary, Queen of Scots, by Elizabeth in 1588, James's claim became stronger. Unlike his Catholic mother, he was a Protestant and therefore more acceptable to the English. Moreover, James was always supportive of the English

Queen. It is a sign of King James's diplomacy that he was able to play the role of successor so well. From 1586 onwards he received an annual pension from the English crown; even when his mother was executed by the English Queen, he kept his protests to a minimum (in fact he may have been relieved that his Catholic mother no longer posed a threat to his rule).

The other claimants to the English throne were not powerful contenders and lacked charisma, and the general feeling in England was that only James could succeed. James could provide England with a monarch who had proved his worth in his dealings with his Scottish lords. On Elizabeth's death, none of the alternative heirs pressed their claims to the throne, and James VI was proclaimed King of England as James I a few hours after Elizabeth's death.

The accession of the Scottish king to the English throne was not popular but neither was it unpopular. As the king of a reformed Protestant nation, James was attractive to the Puritan faction, who wanted the Church of England to become more reformed. Yet as James's wife, Anne of Denmark, had converted to Catholicism, James was also seen by Catholics as someone who might end their oppression. But neither in England nor in Scotland was the union warmly greeted. And yet it was a remarkable union, because for centuries England and Scotland had been fighting each other, and the English had always looked down on their Scottish neighbours.

Macbeth shows the union of Scotland and England in a positive light. The procession of kings in Act IV, Scene 1 is a deliberate piece of propaganda which supports the union of the two thrones: Banquo's descendants – among them James – were portrayed as the legitimate kings of Scotland; indeed it is often presumed that the last king in the procession represents King James. Moreover, in l. 122 Macbeth refers to the 'future' union of the two countries. Interestingly, in Holinshed's *Chronicles* (cf. 'Shakespeare's sources' below), Banquo is depicted as an accomplice of Macbeth in the murder of Duncan; in *Macbeth* he is referred to as '*true, worthy Banquo*' (I, iv, 54) and '*right-valiant Banquo*' (III, vi, 5). So Shakespeare flatters King James through his sympathetic portrait of his 'ancestor'. (It should be noted that most commentators agree that there never was such a person as Banquo.)

In another suggestion of the union of the two nations, Shakespeare stresses how the Scottish lords find refuge in England, and how the English and Scots unite as brothers in arms to remove the tyrant Macbeth.

While Shakespeare is flattering King James by his political allusions in *Macbeth*, he is also reinforcing the political status quo by warning about the chaos that might follow the removal of a rightful monarch. Considering that the fear of chaos is often alluded to in Shakespeare's plays and that *Macbeth* was performed shortly after the Gunpowder Plot of 1605, it can be assumed that Shakespeare's support for the Stuart dynasty was due to the desire for peace that results from a stable political settlement.

James and Witchcraft

Macbeth reflects the way in which James's smooth accession to the English throne and the continuation of political stability and order were broadly welcomed; not only was the natural order retained, but peace seemed guaranteed. The opposite of peace was not really war, but chaos. In *Macbeth* chaos is reflected in the use of witchcraft and the disruption of the **natural order**, both of which are linked in the play to regicide.

Despite the reputation of the Renaissance as a time in which learning and the philosophy of humanism gained importance, there was still considerable superstition; belief in witchcraft was deeply ingrained, even among educated people. Witchcraft was viewed as an attempt to overthrow the natural order established by God, and thus an attempt to overthrow the natural order of mankind. As the monarch was at the head of the political order, witchcraft was believed to be aimed towards removing the king. Throughout Shakespeare's life, fear and persecution of witches was widespread. Hundreds of women (and some men) were executed, often because they used herbal medicines, were old and had cats. It was believed that they kept a 'familiar' in the shape of an animal which allowed the Devil to suck their blood, and they were therefore examined for 'the Devil's marks'.

It was widely believed that any form of treason was connected with the supernatural: 'For rebellion is as the sin of witchcraft,' states the King James edition of the Bible (1 Samuel 15.23) (which besides

Shakespeare's works remains one of the literacy legacies of James's reign). James was so worried by witchcraft that he wrote a tract called *Daemonologie* (1597) to persuade sceptics of the dangers of witchcraft; he even maintained that it was blasphemy not to believe that witches communicated with spirits. In 1604 James made witchcraft a capital crime.

Besides the role of the witches, who undoubtedly would have captured James's interest, there are particular references in the lines of the witches which would have struck a personal chord with the king. In Act I, Scene 3, the witches describe how they control winds and sail in a sieve. These lines refer directly to events in James's own life: James VI of Scotland married Princess Anne of Denmark by proxy in 1589. She sailed for Scotland, but was driven back by storms which the Danish admiral Peter Munk blamed on witches in Copenhagen. James then went to Denmark himself, and on his return to Scotland in 1590 he too encountered storms at sea, which were subsequently blamed on a group of Scottish witches. James himself took over some of the interrogation of these people and was convinced that they had been trying to kill him by raising storms. An account of the affair was published in England, called *Newes from Scotland* (1592). Many of the lines of the witches in *Macbeth* have their origins in this account, as well as in other popular superstitions about witches. When tortured, one of the witches declared that she had collected poison from a toad, christened a cat, sailed out to sea in a sieve and raised a storm to sink the king's ship: '*in a sieve I'll thither sail*'; '*though his bark cannot be lost, Yet it shall be tempest-tossed*' (I, iii, 7 and 22–23)

James presides over the interogation of Scottish witches

Moreover, after the Earl of Gowrie's attempt to kidnap James, it was announced that his bag had been 'full of magical characters' and spells.

So whereas today the witches are almost regarded as comic figures, in Shakespeare's time they would have been seen as dangerous creatures who were part and parcel of chaos; as such, they fitted very neatly into a play about the natural order being upset through the murder of a king, who is God's anointed on earth (another of James's favourite themes). It is, however, worth noting that the witches contribute little to the action; their role is to prophesy, not to cause events. One can, however, argue to what extent they provoke Macbeth into committing murder.

While *Macbeth* has found new resonance with succeeding generations, it is a play which clearly reflects Shakespeare's world and the beliefs and anxieties of his contemporaries, while offering much that would have been of direct interest to King James.

Revision
(what you learn in this section)

- Shakespeare was writing at a time when political stability was not taken for granted. In much of his writing he implies that an attack on the natural order (e.g. through regicide and revolt) will be reflected in chaos in the natural world.
- King James was Shakespeare's patron and God's anointed ruler, so Shakespeare flatters King James through one of the first plays he wrote after James became King of England.
- Shakespeare makes reference to James in the following ways:
  1. He sets the play in Scotland.
  2. One of the 'good' characters is Banquo, supposedly James's ancestor.
  3. He shows the evils of witchcraft.
  4. He comments favourably on the union of England and Scotland.
  5. He refers to the practice of healing people who have scrofula.
  6. He supports the idea of a king being chosen by God, which makes the murder of a monarch a crime against God.

The Theatre

The Globe Theatre

While drama existed in the Middle Ages as mystery and morality plays performed either in church or in processions around town or on wagons that toured from town to town, there were no buildings that one could call 'theatres'. During the 15th and 16th centuries actors would often build built wooden platforms in the courtyards of enclosed inns. The audience could watch from the covered balconies that ran around the courtyard. However, audiences were usually rowdy and there were fights and disturbances, and so actors gained a bad reputation and were indeed subject to arrest if found touring. So some troupes attached themselves to noblemen. They could then travel freely when not needed at court, earning income from and providing entertainment for the general public. These were the first professional companies. They were made up of men and boys only. Women were not allowed to act. Boys played the female roles until their voices changed.

As the city of London started regulating the activities of inns, so acting companies were forced to build their own theatres outside London. The first permanent public theatre was built in 1576 by Richard Burbage; it was called simply 'The Theatre'. It followed the pattern of an inn yard, with a roof open to the sky and a platform surrounded by seats. The theatres in which Shakespeare's plays were first performed – the Theatre, the Curtain and later the Globe – were all of a similar type ('this wooden O', as the theatre is called in the Prologue to *Henry V*). However, as Shakespeare also wrote for the court, many of his plays would have been performed indoors in a hall.

An invitation to perform at court was worth more in money and prestige than many full houses.

The public theatre's stage was relatively small (about 14 metres across and about 9 metres deep) and projected out into the audience; it was called an 'apron' stage and was little more than a metre above the ground, so that 'asides' like Macbeth's, which seem artificial in large modern theatres, could be addressed quite intimately to the audience. The richer members of the audience were seated in three tiered galleries, protected from the weather by a thatched roof, while the rest watched the performance standing in the area around and in front of the stage, and were thus known as the 'groundlings'. If it rained, both actors and groundlings got wet, and this is also true at the reconstructed Globe in London today.

Above the main acting area was an overhanging balcony, which could represent a bedroom window or the battlements of a castle. The actors' entrances and exits were made from doors at the back of the stage, from a curtained area below the balcony, or for sudden appearances and disappearances, through a trapdoor in the floor.

Costumes were generally quite elaborate, though always contemporary, so that *Macbeth*, though set in 11th century Scotland, would have been performed in 17th century costume, and this convention is often referred to today as a justification for so-called 'modern dress' productions. Scenery was minimal, and although there were sound effects and music, there was no artificial lighting, and it was the dialogue that gave the audience essential information about where and when the action was taking place.

The text of *Macbeth*, like all of Shakespeare's plays, includes very few stage directions, but we can see that a bell was rung to announce Duncan's murder, and trumpets were blown and drums beaten for the battle scenes, and we can assume that there were sound effects for the thunder whenever the witches appeared. Everything else had to be conveyed to the audience through the language of the play. For example, the witches establish a sense of place – and weather – when they speak of hovering '*through the fog and filthy air*' (I, i, 13). By contrast, the brief dialogue between Duncan and Banquo (I, vi) creates an impression of a (deceptively) tranquil and harmonious setting.

Since performances all took place in daylight, time and duration also had to be expressed through language. The exchange between Banquo and Fleance which precedes the murder of Duncan is a good example:

BANQUO: How goes the night, boy?
FLEANCE: The moon is down; I have not heard the clock.
BANQUO: And she goes down at twelve.
FLEANCE: I take't, 'tis later, sir
(II, i, 1–3)

This very commonplace discussion gives the audience information about the time and the darkness of the night, as well as setting up the threatening atmosphere for the murder.

As there was no possibility of a blackout in Shakespeare's theatre, and no curtains to draw across the stage, scenes could not easily open with a large number of characters on stage, and this explains why so many scenes begin with two or three characters talking, who are then joined by others. The banquet scene in *Macbeth* does not have to follow this convention, as it is quite natural in this situation for a large group of characters to enter together. Exits, too, were problematic when characters were killed, which is one explanation for so many deaths taking place off stage. The killing of Macduff's son is an exception (though we may assume that the dying child must stagger off stage, mortally wounded), and this makes this particular killing even more shocking.

We also need to remember that since women were not allowed to perform in the theatre, all the female roles in Shakespeare's plays would have been played by young male actors. So when Banquo says to the witches, '*you should be women, And yet your beards forbid me to interpret that you are so*' (I, iii, 43–45), this was perhaps a line designed to please the groundlings, who would have been close enough to notice some dark shadows on the actors' faces.

Apart from the necessary convention of men playing women's roles, we have hardly any evidence of the performance style in Shakespeare's theatre, and we can only speculate about such matters as the pace of the productions and whether the acting was realistic or melodramatic.

Given the conditions in the theatre, with the groundlings moving around and probably responding vocally at times to the action on stage, it is likely that the actors would have had to deliver their lines in loud voices with very clear enunciation. There is also some evidence in the length of many scenes that the plays were often quite static, with periodic bouts of physical action (e.g. sword fights) to hold the interest of the groundlings. Again, though, the texts themselves offer us some clues, at least to their author's probable intentions, if not to the actors' interpretations. In a key scene in *Macbeth*, for example, immediately after Duncan has been killed, the dialogue between Macbeth and Lady Macbeth (II, ii, 13–24) consists of a swift exchange of short, staccato phrases, quite unlike anything in the rest of the play. Here, the style of the writing almost forces the actors to deliver the lines at a rapid, breathless pace, which is appropriate to the whispered conversation of two murderers fearing the discovery of their crime.

English Renaissance Drama

16th-century English drama grew out of the mystery and morality plays of the Middle Ages. While mystery plays tried to make the Christian religion more real by dramatizing key events in the Bible, morality plays used allegory to depict the struggle between the forces of good and evil to possess men's souls. Both types of plays, which were presented on religious festival days, contained a fair amount of humour.

By the end of the 15th century, mystery and morality plays had evolved into secular pieces called 'interludes' that were presented at court dinners. Under Elizabeth, interludes ventured into the political arena. In these more serious interludes lay the seeds of the great tragedies and history plays that would follow.

However, 16th-century drama was also influenced by Ancient Greek and Roman drama, which during the Renaissance started to be read and taught in England. During this period, the subject matter for plays also changed. Where the subject matter of medieval drama was almost always religious, now the focus was upon humanity with all its faults, weaknesses and strengths. Playwrights frequently took their inspiration from Classical models, e.g. the comedies of Plautus, the tragedies of Seneca.

Macbeth can be seen as deriving from both the medieval and Classical drama forms. Elements of the morality play can be seen in the fact that the story of Macbeth is a warning to anybody who considers trying to get what they want by doing something they know is wrong. It also cautions the audience against giving in to temptation: the supernatural forces trick Macbeth into following his ambition, while Lady Macbeth acts as a temptress persuading Macbeth that an evil murder must be done. Moreover, the porter (Act II, Scene 3) would be recognized as a figure from a morality play – the gatekeeper of hell who admits Christ to limbo after his death on the cross. The Porter unwittingly compares Macbeth's castle to hell, and leaves no doubt about the terrible evil of Macbeth's action.

From the tragedies of Seneca emerged the 'revenge tragedy', which became very popular, as did the structure of the five-act play, while many of the elements from his plays, e.g. ghosts, revenge, messengers bringing bad news of death, were incorporated into Elizabethan drama. However, while murders in Seneca's plays happened off stage, the Elizabethan playwrights preferred to show bloodshed on the stage. *Macbeth* is unusual in this, in that only the murder of Lady Macduff and her son are shown.

Revision
(what you learn in this section)

- Drama and theatres were relatively new developments in England.
- Staging a play was not easy, as there were many limitations: lighting was a problem, women were not allowed to act, the audience could be disruptive.
- Shakespeare's dramas took elements from both the medieval morality play and Classical drama.

Shakespeare's Sources

Shakespeare did not invent most of his stories. He usually based his plays on already existing accounts, stories, poems or indeed other plays. When King James became king and patron of his acting company, Shakespeare must have considered it advisable and profitable to write a play set in Scotland that dealt with kingship (and touched on the present King).

Shakespeare may have chosen the story of Macbeth as it recalled the attack on King James by the Earl of Gowrie, which took place while James was Gowrie's guest (cf. 'King James', above, p. 11).

But Shakespeare drew most of his information from Holinshed's *Chronicles of England, Scotland and Ireland* (1577), which had been reprinted in 1587 and had provided much of the material for Shakespeare's earlier history plays. Holinshed's information was itself taken from other books and accounts. In Holinshed's *Chronicles*, Shakespeare found the history of a medieval Scottish king, Macbeth, which is the story of a murderous lord and his ambitious wife. However, to make his play more dramatic, Shakespeare also drew on Holinshed's story of the murder of King Duff by Donwald. It is Duff who was killed while he was a guest of his murderer.

Shakespeare used his sources freely, adding and removing characters and action to suit his own dramatic purposes. *Macbeth* is a play with no subplot and with remarkably few characters for its time. The sources were plundered for their essence – the theme of regicide and the destruction of a man by ambition.

Holinshed writes of Macbeth's good first ten years as a ruler, but Shakespeare ignored the political background in Holinshed's stories. He makes Macbeth a more inherently evil character and at the same time makes King Duncan more pious and holy. This would have pleased King James, to whom regicide was an act against a divinely appointed ruler.

As mentioned above (cf. 'The Union of Two Nations', p. 12), Shakespeare ignores Holinshed's depiction of Banquo as a co-conspirator with Macbeth in the death of Duncan. Far more important is the detailed family tree of the Stuart dynasty going back to Banquo which Holinshed included in his *Chronicles*. In *Macbeth* the reference to Banquo's descendant King James is made clear in the procession of kings (IV, i, 111–123).

While Shakespeare invented Lady Macbeth's sleepwalking and death, the character of Lady Macbeth is actually a composite of different characters in Holinshed's *Chronicles*. Holinshed says of Lady Macbeth that she was an ambitious wife: 'burning in unquenchable desire to bear the name of a queen.' But Shakespeare's 'fiend-like queen' has much in common with Fenella, the murderer of King Kenneth. And Donwald's wife also urges him to kill King Duff. With three Scottish women ready to commit murder or to urge their husbands on, Shakespeare had a lot of material to choose from.

King Kenneth was also a murderer and, according to Holinshed, suffered from guilt and lack of sleep – key themes in Macbeth.

So much of what we find in *Macbeth* is adapted from other sources.

The Real Macbeth

The Scottish king, Macbeth, whose life is described by Holinshed, lived in the 11th century. He was born in 1005 into a turbulent nation of tribal factions and brutal fighting. While ruling families fought each other for power, the country was being attacked by the Vikings and Norsemen. Macbeth's father ruled the province of Moray and Ross, and was killed by his nephews. Macbeth became later ruler of Moray and Ross and then killed King Duncan, an unpopular and ineffective ruler, in battle. Macbeth had a legitimate claim to the throne as he, like Duncan, was a grandson of King Malcolm II. In the 11th century, the kings of Scotland were elected by their fellow lords (thanes). Macbeth was elected by the thanes to be High King of Scotland and ruled from 1040 to 1057. He was succeeded by Duncan's son, Malcolm.

Unlike Shakespeare's evil tyrant, the actual King Macbeth was a respected ruler, and the first ten years of his reign, in particular, were noted for giving Scotland a period of peace and relative prosperity. He was married to Gruoch, grand-daughter of King Kenneth III, a union that enhanced his claim to the throne. There is no indication that they had any children and nothing is known about the real Lady Macbeth. During the later years of his rule, King Macbeth became unpopular and was killed in battle by Malcolm. He was buried at Iona, the sacred burial place for the kings of Scotland.

Revision
(what you learn in this section)

- Shakespeare did not invent most of his stories; he adapted stories he had read and turned them into dramatic tales.
- His main source for Macbeth was Holinshed's *Chronicles of England, Scotland and Ireland*.
- Shakespeare changed some details, e.g. Banquo is not Macbeth's accomplice in Duncan's murder, as Banquo was believed to be James's ancestor.
- The real King Macbeth was a lot better than the character depicted in Macbeth.

Reception

Macbeth has been regarded by some as Shakespeare's greatest play. The Romantic poet Samuel Taylor Coleridge noted its absence of comedy or even irony and philosophic contemplation, and called it 'wholly tragic'. Early 20th century poet John Masefield said it was the 'most glorious' of Shakespeare's plays and one 19th century critic wrote that *Macbeth* was 'the greatest treasure of our dramatic literature'. But the play has also been Shakespeare's most criticized, particularly by literary critics, many of whom feel that its brevity and the abruptness of some scenes are clear signs that much of the text is missing. Many contemporary critics feel that the Folio text (which is the basis for all editions of *Macbeth*) is a combination of at least two versions, with the main part originating from the time of the Gunpowder plot with sections (e.g. Act III, Scene 5), being added later by Thomas Middleton. Others feel that this text is an early version, with additional parts added for a production before King James.

We have no proof of any of this, nor do we have any reports of the first performances, which are thought to have been before King James. The King had given Shakespeare's company of actors, The Lord Chamberlain's Men, royal patronage, making them The King's Men, and they probably performed *Macbeth* at court in 1606. We know little, too, about how the play was received at the time. The only review we have from the period is by an astrologer, Simon Forman, who describes seeing the play at the Globe Theatre in 1611.

While *Macbeth* was frequently produced, it was often regarded as difficult, and it was the intensity of the play – the unrelenting tragedy noted by Coleridge – that caused many producers over the years to feel that it needed re-writing. When the diarist Samuel Pepys saw *Macbeth* in the 1660s, he found it 'a most excellent play in all respects, especially in divertisement, though it be a deep tragedy'. The *Macbeth* he saw was not the play we see today. Songs and dances were added to entertain the audience of the day, who had been deprived of theatre and entertainment under the Commonwealth and Protectorate (1642–1660).

Sir William Davenant (1606–1668), Shakespeare's godson, was responsible for most of the 17th century productions of Shakespeare, and it would have been his version that Pepys saw. He cut out the Porter and the Doctor, made Seyton change sides at the end, inserted a new scene with Lady Macbeth and Lady Macduff, and allowed the witches to dance, sing and fly. These productions, said one angry critic of the period, turned Shakespeare into pantomime. Davenant also commissioned what is known as 'the Macbeth music' (often thought to have been written by Purcell) for a performance in 1672. A song for Hecate and some of the witches' songs may have been written for this production. This version suited the new theatres of the period, which now used a proscenium stage, demanding a greater emphasis on scenery. (A proscenium stage is one that is set behind an arch so that the audience all sit in front of the stage facing it.) The tastes of the time also required the newly invented machines which created stage effects, and music and dance to relieve the mood.

In 1744, the great actor David Garrick produced *Macbeth* 'as written by William Shakespeare', though many scenes were cut and he wrote a long dying speech for Macbeth. In the 19th century the audiences wanted naturalism: the stage was filled with Gothic castles and, in one production, over 100 witches.

It was not until the beginning of the 20th century that William Poel, who believed that the most important things were Shakespeare's words and the poetry, removed the clutter on stage and returned to Shakepeare's text. Naturalism and flying witches have now been replaced by a return to the text and minimal scenery.

Contemporary productions have also centred on the essence of the tragedy and the violence of the history it portrays. It is this which has also featured most strongly in foreign versions of the play, which have removed it from its setting and allowed it to reinvent itself in a wide variety of geographical locations, with Scotland becoming a European dictatorship or a war zone in Africa. Most film versions have also freely interpreted the play, from Akira Kurosawa's *Throne of Blood* (1957), an adaptation set in the Japan of the samurai, to Roman Polanski's 1971 film, which was greatly influenced by his own tragic family history (his pregnant wife and four friends were brutally murdered by the 'Manson Family' in 1969).

Contemporary audiences also demand productions that are centred on the psychology of the characters. One might say that the greatness of *Macbeth* can be seen in the way in which it can be adapted to suit the changing tastes of different periods. It has remained one of the most produced plays in the history of the theatre, and its continuing influence can be seen in the fact that in 2005 twenty members of the Scottish Parliament put forward a petition calling for an ‘amnesty’ for Macbeth and a ban on productions of the play in Scotland, so that the reputation of the historical king could be rescued from the image created by Shakespeare.

The Story

The play is set in 11th century Scotland. There has been a revolt against Duncan, the King, led by two thanes (Scottish noblemen), Cawdor and Macdonald, who are supported by the King of Norway.

Act I

Scene 1

The play opens on some battlefield or heath with thunder and lightning.

What atmosphere is conjured up by the setting?

Three witches appear, and it is clear from the first line ('*When shall we three meet again?*') that the play starts at the end of their meeting.

They intend to meet Macbeth '*when the battle's lost and won*'. In a dozen short lines, full of strange paradoxes, they establish an atmosphere of a world turned upside down, where '*fair is foul, and foul is fair*'.

Their dialogue is written in rhyming tetrameters

Scene 2

In the royal camp, King Duncan and his eldest son, Malcolm, receive a report of the bravery in battle of Banquo and Macbeth.

Their first description we hear of Macbeth is of his brutal killing of Macdonald, whom he has almost split in two and decapitated.

This is the second time we hear about Macbeth, but we have still not met him.

Duncan receives a further report of the rebels' defeat and surrender. He orders Cawdor's execution and confers Cawdor's title on Macbeth.

Scene 3

The three witches meet on a heath; they speak about their magical powers and their unnatural deeds.

Macbeth and Banquo appear, and the Witches hail Macbeth as Thane of Glamis, Thane of Cawdor and '*king hereafter*'. They tell Banquo that he will not be a king, but that his descendants will be kings. Macbeth demands to know more, but the witches vanish.

Note Macbeth's first words. What do they remind you of?

Notice how the witches use confusing language in their prophecies (ll. 63–65).

Banquo thinks they have been hallucinating, while Macbeth's first thought is of the prophecy that Banquo will be the father of kings.

Almost immediately, Ross and Angus, two thanes, greet Macbeth as Thane of Cawdor. Macbeth and Banquo are amazed at the fulfilment of the witches' first prophecy. Macbeth is already troubled by thoughts of murder, but hopes that it might simply be his good fortune to become King without having to take any action.

Scene 4

In the royal palace, Malcolm describes Cawdor's execution to Duncan. Before his death, Cawdor had repented and begged for the King's forgiveness. Duncan names Malcolm as his successor to the throne.

Here the old Thane of Cawdor is discussed as the new one arrives. Why might this be ironic?

Macbeth declares his loyalty and obedience to the King, but in an aside he sees Malcolm as a further obstacle on his path to the throne, and admits to his '*deep and black desires*'. Duncan announces his intention to visit Macbeth's castle, and Macbeth leaves in advance to inform his wife and make preparations for their royal guest.

Scene 5

Lady Macbeth learns about the witches' prophecies in a letter from her husband, and instantly begins to think about how he might take the throne. She does not share Macbeth's doubts and hesitation, and she fears that her husband may not

This scene tells us a lot about Lady Macbeth, Macbeth and their relationship.

have the courage to act. But she is determined to persuade him of what they need to do. When Macbeth returns with news of the King's imminent arrival, she puts into words what they have each been thinking about – the murder of Duncan.

Scene 6

Duncan, accompanied by Malcolm, Banquo and the other thanes, arrives at Macbeth's castle. Unsuspecting, the King praises the pleasant atmosphere around the castle. Lady Macbeth welcomes Duncan, apparently as loyal as her husband, but describing their service to the King as being '*done double*'.

This is an example of dramatic irony. Duncan arrives at Macbeth's castle and praises its pleasantness. Unlike the audience, he is unaware of the fact that the Macbeths intend to murder him.

Scene 7

Alone, Macbeth considers the possibility of murdering the King. He wavers between his determination to act swiftly and his fear of the consequences of his actions. Duncan is his guest and a relative as well as his king, and Macbeth is afraid of being punished for the terrible crime of regicide. His wife enters, and when Macbeth tells her he has decided not to go ahead with their plan, she provokes him to action by challenging his manhood. She has none of Macbeth's misgivings and rejects her feminine nature; while he has been tormented by his conscience, she has been thinking about exactly how they can commit the murder. Her plan is to get the King's grooms drunk, and for her husband to incriminate them by using their daggers to kill their master. Macbeth adds a further refinement: they will smear the grooms with the King's blood. By the end of the scene Macbeth has decided to act.

This is a key scene for appreciating the differences between Macbeth and Lady Macbeth.

Act II

Scene 1

Act II opens some time after midnight in the inner courtyard of Macbeth's castle. Banquo and his son, Fleance, are on guard. Banquo is still disturbed by the witches' strange prophecies, and when Macbeth enters, he starts to tell him how he has dreamed about the witches. But Macbeth dismisses the subject, pretending that he has not been thinking about it. Banquo and Fleance leave, and Macbeth, left alone, sees a dagger hanging in the air with its handle pointing towards him. Unsure whether the dagger is real or a hallucination, he tries to grab it, and when he fails, the dagger suddenly appears to be dripping with blood. Finally, he decides that the dagger must be a vision caused by his thoughts of murder. Despite his fear of being discovered, he tells himself that as long as he delays, Duncan will still remain alive. He decides to go ahead with the killing, and hearing a bell toll, he says it is calling Duncan to heaven or to hell.

How might a theatre production depict this dagger?

Scene 2

The scene continues in the inner courtyard, as Lady Macbeth enters. She has drugged the grooms who were guarding Duncan, but left their daggers for Macbeth to kill the King. The murder takes place off stage, and Macbeth enters, simply announcing to his wife that he has '*done the deed*', but still carrying the murder weapons which he was supposed to have left beside the grooms so as to incriminate them. He explains how on overhearing the grooms' prayers, he was unable to respond '*Amen*', and then heard a voice crying '*Sleep no more! Macbeth does murder sleep*'. Lady

Note how the murder is accompanied by a bird of ill omen and how Macbeth is unable to pray.

Macbeth tries to reassure him, and urges him to return with the daggers, but paralysed with fear, he flatly refuses. Once again, she shows herself to be more pragmatic and strong-minded than her husband, and she takes the daggers, instructing Macbeth to wash the blood from his hands. As soon as she leaves the stage, a noise of knocking begins, which continues until the end of the scene. Macbeth becomes increasingly panic-stricken, and when his wife returns with her hands as bloody as his, she takes control of the situation, saying that they should both wash their hands and go to bed, so that no one will suspect them of the murder. Macbeth is immediately filled with regret, wishing that the knocking could awaken Duncan.

Note how twice Lady Macbeth refers to washing away the blood (even commenting 'how easy it is').

Scene 3

This scene, still set in the inner courtyard, begins with the only piece of comic relief in the play: a drunken porter enters and delays opening the gate to the castle, imagining himself to be the gatekeeper to Hell welcoming a parade of sinners. The knocking continues relentlessly throughout his speech. He finally opens the gate to admit Macduff and Lennox, who have been commanded by the King to come early in the morning to Macbeth's castle. They joke with the Porter about the effects of alcohol until Macbeth enters, pretending that he has only just woken up. Macduff goes to see the King, and while he is offstage, Lennox tells Macbeth about the previous night's storm and various superstitious rumours of death and destruction. Macduff returns with the news that the King has been murdered. Hardly able to believe what has happened, he tells Macbeth and Lennox to go and see for themselves. An alarm bell is sounded, and Banquo and Lady Macbeth

The porter makes reference to equivocation and the Gunpowder Plot (cf. pp. 7–8).

Yet more omens of ill fortune are mentioned.

enter. On being told of the murder, her first reaction is to express her disbelief that such a thing could have happened '*in our house*'. Macbeth and Lennox return, followed by the King's sons, Malcolm and Donalbain. Macbeth tells them indirectly about their father's murder, using an image of the source of their blood, leaving Macduff to say plainly, '*Your royal father's murdered*'. Lennox reports on the apparent guilt of the grooms, who have been killed by Macbeth. When Macduff asks why he did this, Macbeth pretends to have been overcome with anger and emotion. At this point, Lady Macbeth faints and is carried out. Everyone leaves the stage except Malcolm and Donalbain. Fearing that they might be the next victims, they plan to leave Scotland. They decide that it will be safer to choose separate destinations, with Donalbain going to Ireland while Malcolm travels to England.

Do you think Lady Macbeth is acting or did she really faint?

Scene 4

Outside the castle, Ross talks to an old man about strange, unnatural events that have taken place on the night of Duncan's murder (a falcon killed by an owl, Duncan's horses breaking loose and eating each other). Macduff enters with the news that the King's sons have fled, which convinces him that they had employed the grooms to kill their father. In the absence of Malcolm and Donalbain, Macbeth has already been named as the new king. Macduff is uneasy and tells Ross he will not attend Macbeth's coronation.

(And once again) regicide is accompanied by unnatural events.

Act III

Scene 1

The scene opens in Macbeth's castle. Alone on stage, Banquo is beginning to suspect that Macbeth may have made the final prophecy come true by killing Duncan. But he also recalls the witches' other prophecy that his descendants (though not he himself) will be kings of Scotland. Macbeth and Lady Macbeth enter, dressed in their coronation robes, with Lennox and Ross. Macbeth invites Banquo to the coronation feast, then asks if he plans to spend the afternoon riding. He also wants to know how far Banquo intends to ride and whether his son, Fleance, will ride with him. Everyone leaves except for Macbeth. While Macbeth has put the blame for Duncan's murder on Malcolm and Donalbain, he is troubled by the thought that it is Banquo's descendants and not his who will inherit the throne. He meets with two murderers and having convinced them that Banquo is their enemy, orders them to kill Banquo and Fleance, and to make sure that this is done well away from the palace.

Now that his prophecies have been fulfilled, Macbeth turns his thoughts to those about Banquo.

Scene 2

The banquet is about to take place. Lady Macbeth reproaches her husband for his weakness and anxiety, telling him '*what's done is done*'. She tries to encourage Macbeth to be '*bright and jovial*' for their guests, but he is preoccupied by the threat to the throne from Banquo and Fleance. Macbeth hints to his wife that he has made arrangements to have them removed, but he does not want to give her any details until he has solved the problem.

Scene 3

In a park near the palace, the two murderers are joined by a third, and together they ambush Banquo and Fleance. Banquo is killed, but in the darkness Fleance manages to escape.

Scene 4

Macbeth and Lady Macbeth welcome Lennox, Ross and the other guests to their banquet. As the guests sit down, one of the murderers arrives and informs Macbeth of what has happened. Macbeth congratulates him on Banquo's killing, but is deeply troubled by the news that Fleance is still alive. When Macbeth returns to the table, he finds Banquo's bloodstained ghost sitting in his place. No one else can see the ghost, and they assume that Macbeth is ill. The ghost vanishes, and Macbeth recovers, asking his guests to forgive his strange behaviour. But then the ghost reappears. It disappears a second time, but now Macbeth is so badly frightened that Lady Macbeth asks everyone to leave. Alone with his wife, Macbeth tells her that Macduff has refused to attend the banquet. Suspecting another threat to his security, he decides to go back to the witches to try to find out what else is going to happen. He sees himself as halfway across a river of blood, at the point where it would be as difficult to go back as to go on, and in the last line of the scene ('*We are but young in deed*') he suggests that there will be more killing to come.

Consider how the ghost might appear in a production of *Macbeth*. Notice how Macbeth sees Banquo both times after he has spoken about him and his absence.

Scene 5

In another storm, the witches meet Hecate, goddess of the underworld and Queen of the Witches. She rebukes them for acting independently and not including her in their dealings with

Scholars are usually in agreement that this scene was not written by Shakespeare but was added later.

Macbeth, particularly since he is driven by personal ambition and not by love for them. She tells them how she plans to deceive Macbeth, so that he will think he is invincible.

Scene 6

Lennox discusses recent events with another nobleman. In a heavily ironic speech, Lennox catalogues the murders of Duncan and Banquo (‘*men must not walk too late*’), Macbeth’s sudden slaughter of the grooms (‘*How it did grieve Macbeth!*’), the accusations against Malcolm and Donalbain, and Macduff’s offence in refusing to attend the coronation banquet. The nobleman informs Lennox that Macduff has gone to England, where he and Malcolm, with support from King Edward, are gathering an army to overthrow Macbeth and restore peace and prosperity to Scotland.

Act IV

Scene 1

In a cave, once again announced by thunder, the witches chant over a boiling cauldron, listing all the disgusting ingredients for their magic spell. Hecate joins them briefly and compliments them on their work. Macbeth arrives, and demands to be told more. They make three ghosts appear to tell him what he wants to know. The first ghost, an armed head **a**, warns Macbeth to ‘*Beware the thane of Fife*’ (Macduff); the second, a bloodstained child **b**, tells him that he will never be harmed by anyone ‘*of woman born*’; the third, a child wearing a crown **c**, tells him he will never be beaten in battle until Birnam Wood comes to Dunsinane. Macbeth is reassured by these last two prophecies, which seem to offer him absolute security, but

a This head might represent Macduff.

b This may also represent Macduff, who – it is later revealed – was torn from his mother’s womb.

c This may represent future kings (e.g. Banquo’s descendants) who rule after Birnam Wood moved to Dunsinane (after which Macbeth was defeated).

mindful of the warning from the first ghost, vows to kill Macduff, so as to be absolutely sure he is safe. When Macbeth then insists on knowing if Banquo's descendants will rule in Scotland, a procession of eight ghostly kings appears, followed by the ghost of Banquo. The ghosts and the witches disappear. Lennox enters, and when Macbeth asks him if he has seen the witches, he swears he has not. He brings Macbeth the news that Macduff has fled to England. Macbeth's reaction is swift and brutal: he determines to kill Macduff's wife and children.

Banquo's descendants included King James: the eight kings may represent the Stuart monarchs while the mirror shows the descendants through the ages.

Scene 2

In Macduff's castle, Lady Macduff tells Ross, her cousin, that she cannot understand her husband's decision to leave his wife and family unprotected. Ross tries to persuade her that Macduff has acted wisely, but she remains unconvinced. Ross leaves, afraid for his own safety, and Lady Macduff tells her young son that his father is dead. As she is not crying, the child does not believe her, but is troubled by the idea that Macduff has been condemned as a traitor. A messenger arrives and warns her that she and her children are in danger and that they should leave the castle at once. The messenger exits, afraid to stay any longer, and Lady Macduff, left alone, is afraid that although she has done nothing wrong, her innocence may not save her. The murderers break in. Macduff's son is stabbed and Lady Macduff runs off, with the murderers in pursuit.

Scene 3

Macduff has arrived at the English court, and meets with Malcolm. Malcolm is cautious at first, reminding Macduff that in the past Macbeth was loved and trusted by Duncan and by Macduff himself. Malcolm also makes the point that Macduff does not share his personal motive for revenge ('*He hath not touched you yet*'). Malcolm then tests Macduff by pretending that if he was king, he would outdo Macbeth in wickedness and cruelty, so that '*black Macbeth will seem as pure as snow*'. Macduff is horrified at this false confession, and is about to leave, swearing that he will never return to Scotland, when Malcolm reveals his trick and explains why he felt he needed to test Macduff's loyalty and morality. He assures Macduff that this is the first time he has ever told a lie, and tells him they will join the army of ten thousand men raised by Siward, Malcolm's uncle, to march on Scotland and reclaim the throne. Macduff initially finds it difficult to accept Malcolm's sudden change of character ('*Such welcome and unwelcome things at once 'tis hard to reconcile.*'). A doctor brings news of King Edward's gift for healing victims of 'the Evil' (the disease scrofula). Ross arrives with the latest reports from Scotland. At first, he only talks about the general state of the country, and when Macduff asks for news of his family, Ross delays telling him the truth, saying that they are '*at peace*'. Macduff urges him to speak more clearly, and without describing the details, he finally tells him of the murders. Macduff is overcome with grief and guilt at having abandoned his family, but as Malcolm encourages him to seek revenge, he resolves personally to kill Macbeth, and together with Ross, they leave to join with Siward's forces.

Malcolm lists the virtues a king should possess in ll. 92–94.

Act V

Scene 1

In Macbeth's castle at Dunsinane, a doctor has been called by a gentlewoman to witness Lady Macbeth sleepwalking. The gentlewoman refuses to report what she has heard Lady Macbeth saying, and insists on the doctor hearing it for himself. Lady Macbeth appears, obsessively rubbing her hands as if she is washing them, and speaking incoherently about her guilt and the blood on her hands. In her semi-conscious state, she refers to the murders of Duncan ('*Who would have thought the old man to have had so much blood in him?*'), Lady Macduff ('*The thane of Fife had a wife: where is she now?*') and Banquo ('*I tell you yet again, Banquo's buried; he cannot come out on's grave*'). The doctor clearly has little doubt what all this means, but is afraid to tell anyone about it ('*I think, but dare not speak*').

Scene 2

In the countryside near Macbeth's castle, Lennox, Menteith, Caithness and Angus are marching with their soldiers towards Birnam Wood, where they plan to meet Malcolm, Macduff, Siward and the English army. Caithness reports on Macbeth's preparations to defend his castle and his growing instability, while Angus says that Macbeth is increasingly tormented by guilt, and that his followers only continue to obey him out of fear. The thanes are determined to defeat Macbeth and 'heal' Scotland's sickness.

Scene 3

In the castle, Macbeth ignores reports of the advancing army, reassuring himself with the witches' predictions that '*no man that's born of woman*' can kill him and that he will not be defeated until Birnam Wood comes to Dunsinane. For a moment, he reflects on his loss of honour and friendship, but then calls for his armour, swearing to fight until he is killed and ordering anyone who speaks of fear to be hanged. The doctor tells Macbeth that his wife is suffering from insomnia and hallucinations. Macbeth would like the doctor to cure her sick mind by removing the memories that trouble her. When the doctor tells him that his patient must cure herself, Macbeth wishes that Scotland could be '*cured*' (though it is the English invasion that he sees as Scotland's sickness).

Scene 4

Near Birnam Wood, the rebel thanes have joined forces with Malcolm and the English army. Malcolm instructs his men to camouflage themselves with branches cut from the trees, so as to disguise their numbers. Siward reports that Macbeth is confidently awaiting their attack even though most of his followers have deserted him. The army marches on towards Dunsinane.

Here the prophecy of Birnam Wood moving is fulfilled.

Scene 5

In the castle, Macbeth is defiantly preparing for a siege when he is interrupted by the sound of women screaming. Unmoved but curious, he sends Seyton, his armour-bearer, to find out what has happened. Seyton returns with the news that Lady Macbeth is dead. Macbeth is barely able to mourn her loss ('*She should have died hereafter; there would have been a time for such a word.*'), but reflects on the brevity and meaninglessness of life ('*a tale told by an idiot, full of sound and fury signifying nothing*'). A messenger arrives to report that he

This is Macbeth's final contemplation on life before he dies: it is pessimistic, as is appropriate to someone facing catastrophe.

has seen Birnam Wood moving towards Dunsinane. Macbeth begins to doubt the witches' promises, and declares himself ready to die fighting.

Scene 6

Malcolm's forces arrive at Dunsinane. He orders his men to throw down their branches and prepare to attack the castle.

Scene 7

Still believing himself to be invincible, Macbeth enters, and after a brief fight, kills Young Siward (Siward's son). In the midst of the fierce battle, Macduff appears, determined to find and kill Macbeth. Siward informs him that Macbeth's men are deserting him and that victory is almost theirs.

Scene 8

Macbeth appears, close to defeat, but unwilling to commit suicide. When challenged by Macduff, he is reluctant to add Macduff's death to those of his wife and children, but Macduff forces him to fight. As they struggle, Macbeth boasts that he cannot be killed by anyone '*of woman born*'. Macduff tells him that he did not have a natural birth, but was 'ripped' prematurely from his mother's womb. Macbeth realizes how the witches have tricked him again, and tries to abandon the fight. Macduff orders him to surrender, which Macbeth refuses to do, and they exit, still fighting.

Scene 9

Siward, informed of his son's death in battle, is proud that the young man has died bravely, with his wounds '*on the front*'. Macduff returns, holding Macbeth's severed head, and hails Malcolm as the new king of Scotland. To express his gratitude for the support he has received from Macduff and the other thanes, Malcolm names them earls, and invites them all to attend his coronation.

The Characters

Macbeth

A warrior, a murderer, a loving husband, a man driven mad by guilt, a tyrant ... Who is Shakespeare's Macbeth?

What we know about Macbeth comes from three sources:

a) what he does;
b) what he says;
c) what other characters say about him.

Our first introduction to Macbeth is through the Captain's report (I, ii). This is a vivid account of a battle in which Macbeth is described as a hero, a **warrior** who 'carves' his way through the enemy forces and when he kills the rebel, Macdonald, almost splits him in two. Macbeth here is portrayed as a **fighter**, a man who comes alive on a bloody battlefield, filled with superhuman energy when the odds seem to be against him. This is a man of war, described as '*brave*' and '*noble*'.

However, our first encounter with Macbeth creates a very different impression. His first words ('*So foul and fair a day I have not seen*', I, iii, 36) are mostly likely his own description of the battle in which foul acts were carried out but resulted in victory. Whatever interpretation is made of them, however, they are **reflective**. They are not the words of a man of action. Thus, we already have a contradiction: **Macbeth acts like a warrior, but talks like a dreamer**. This duality presents a **bold ambitious man of action** who has the **imagination of a poet**. This view of Macbeth accounts for his nervous reaction to the witches' prediction that he will be Thane of Cawdor and '*king hereafter*' (I, iii, 48).

Again, while Macbeth is described as a heroic fighter by others, within 14 lines of his entrance he appears to be a very different kind of man, one whose reaction to good news is to '*start and seem to fear*' (I, iii, 49), a man, it would seem, with a more **active imagination** than Banquo, whose reaction to the witches is more what one might expect of a soldier – practical and incredulous. We sense that Macbeth is already thinking about what he must do to fulfil the witches' predictions. This is confirmed in his first soliloquy where he is pulled in two directions: were the witches' predictions good or evil? One prediction comes true almost immediately: Macbeth is made Thane of Cawdor. But will the kingship fall into his lap without his taking any action? Or does he have to act on the information given to him by the witches and kill Duncan to bring it about?

Throughout Act I the audience is given conflicting information about Macbeth. When Duncan declares that his son Malcolm will inherit the throne, we see Macbeth's ambition and how he may be prepared to take action to get the crown, and yet the description of Macbeth we receive from his wife is that he is '*too full o' the milk of human kindness*' (I, v, 16). This is not a character trait which we would normally associate with an ambitious and ruthless warrior. Lady Macbeth acknowledges his ambition, but is aware that he would prefer to be elected to the throne rather than have to take it illegally, by force. This confirms what we have learned from Macbeth himself: he is a man who prefers not to act unless he is forced to do so, and he is always aware of the possible consequences of his actions. Killing in war, when he is not responsible for the consequences, is not a problem; the consequences of acting outside of war, and outside the law, are in the end what destroy him.

The play is, after all, *The Tragedy of Macbeth* and Shakespeare's tragic heroes all possess a mixture of nobility of courage and some kind of weakness (often called their '**tragic flaw**') which leads to their downfall and destruction. Macbeth's 'tragic flaw' is clearly his ambition. His longing to be king leads him not just to become a murderer, but a host who goes against all the rules of civilized behaviour and kills his own guest. But Macbeth cannot deal with the consequences of this action. **His conscience torments him**; it prevents him from sleeping. He is driven to kill again and again, but even at the moment when he does act and kill Duncan, he is tortured by doubts; he is unable to smear the grooms with the King's blood, as pre-arranged, to implicate them in the murder. As Lady Macbeth observes, '*what thou wouldst highly, that wouldst thou holily*' (I, v, 19–20).

Once he has become king, however, Macbeth feels he must **protect his position** by removing all those who may threaten him: he orders first the murder of Banquo and later that of Macduff's wife and children. He reaches a point, half-way through the play, where he explains the terrible logic of this chain of killings: '*I am in blood stepped in so far that should I wade no more, returning were as tedious as go o'er*' (III, iv, 136–138). From this point onwards, Macbeth stops questioning his actions and becomes increasingly **tyrannical**. By Act V he has become a **hated ruler**, responsible for the brutal repression of his people, deserted by almost all his nobles. His only moment of humanity is when he hears of the death of his wife, and he admits to himself how his character has changed: '*I have almost forgot the taste of fears; the time has been, my senses would have cooled to hear a night-shriek*' (V, v, 9–11). The futility of his life and his actions is finally clear to him. His ambition to become king has made him forget how a king should act, and so he becomes a **loathed tyrant**. So by the end of the play we have seen Macbeth commit great evil:

- He has committed regicide, the worse form of murder; the victim, Duncan, was a relative and a guest, so he has murdered someone of his own blood who was under his protection.
- He has usurped the crown.
- He has the sons of Duncan blamed for the murder.
- He has his best friend, Banquo, murdered.
- He has Lady Macduff and her children murdered.
- He turns Scotland into a miserable country.
- He communicates with evil beings, the witches.

Macbeth and Lady Macbeth are united by passion as well as by ambition: '*My dearest love*', he greets Lady Macbeth when he returns to his castle at Inverness. Macbeth and his wife may be seen as two halves of one character, that one was completed by the other. It is certainly true that in order to obtain the power they desire, they need each other. In the early stages of their plotting, it is Lady Macbeth who urges on her husband and attacks him for his **weakness**, but later in the play, it appears that Macbeth may wish to shield his wife from knowing too much about his actions ('*Be innocent of the knowledge, dearest chuck, till thou applaud the deed*', III, ii, 44–45), though this **protectiveness** is short-lived. After Lady Macbeth's death, Macbeth is reduced to the mindless killing machine described by the Captain at the start of the play: up to his neck in blood, slashing away at his enemies. In his own view of himself, he is no more than a wild animal fighting hopelessly to survive, but knowing he is beaten: '*At least we'll die with harness on our back*' (V, v, 51).

There would be no tragedy, however if this bloodthirsty soldier was our sole image of Macbeth. It is his **battles with his conscience** and the **conflict within him** that make him an interesting character. After he has killed Duncan and Banquo, we see a man **haunted by guilt**, aware that each act he performs to raise himself, further destroys him: '*that we but teach bloody instructions, which, being taught, return to plague the inventor*' (I, vii, 8–10). The murder of Duncan can only be explained by his ambition. It is a cowardly act that he himself knows is wrong. For this reason he appears almost deranged immediately after the murder. With Banquo the reasons are different: he is acting out of fear. Banquo knows of the meeting with the witches and it is children who will become kings of Scotland. Even though he should know that he cannot alter a prophecy, he attempts to do so by murdering the man he sees as a danger and a rival. His actions are necessary to protect his position: '*To be thus is nothing, but to be safely thus*' (III, i, 49–50). But they make him more and more isolated and eventually destroy him.

Increasingly, Macbeth appears to others, and from his own actions, as a villain. The murder of an innocent woman and her children, because they are Macduff's family can only be seen as cruel and vindicative (and the murder of the boy on stage reinforces the brutality of the deed).

But while Macbeth has become a murderer and a tyrant, to the audience he remains an interesting and complex character because of what he reveals about his own feelings. We travel with him as he becomes more and more steeped in blood and we see how this affects him. We are aware of the tragedy of Macbeth.

Macbeth's psychology has frequently been analysed, and his questions to the doctor about the madness that is destroying his wife ('*Canst thou not minister to a mind diseased, pluck from the memory a rooted sorrow, raze out the written troubles of the brain*', V, iii, 41–43) demonstrate an almost modern understanding of psychiatry. It has been observed by doctors how Macbeth's inability to sleep following the murder has much in common with post-traumatic stress disorder. The brutality of medieval Scotland had many echoes in the violence of Elizabethan and

Jacobean England, and must have given Shakespeare many examples to draw upon.

One key to unlocking Macbeth's character lies in how we interpret his actions in terms of the supernatural elements, and this is always a problem when staging the play. If the witches, the dagger, the apparitions and the ghost of Banquo are seen by the audience as real, then Macbeth may be seen to some extent as a **victim of forces beyond his control**, weak perhaps, but powerless to escape his destiny. If, on the other hand, as in many modern productions, the dagger and the ghost are invisible and the witches less magical, Macbeth becomes much more culpable and the supernatural elements are seen as **projections of his secret desires and anxieties**.

However, a modern reader must remember that for most of Shakespeare's audience, only demonic possession could have led a brave soldier to become the killer of a king. This is reflected in Macbeth's inability to pray, by his hallucinations and the changes in his behaviour. Macbeth is vulnerable to these supernatural voices of evil because they tell him what he wants to hear, but they cannot be trusted, and their later riddles prove to be the equivocations (another key theme of the play) that lead him to his destruction. They are, as Banquo realizes, the '*instruments of darkness*' who tell the truth about small matters in order to hide what is important. They are, however, the stimulus that Macbeth needs to push himself on, and when they are not present, it might be said that their role in the play is taken over by Lady Macbeth herself.

Despite his actions, we find a man undergoing a **deep struggle of conscience** and we witness the moral despair that overcomes him. Macbeth is the only character in the play who reveals an inner life, and despite his evil acts, audiences are moved by his fate. He may be a warrior and a murderer, but he is also a loving husband and a complex man driven mad by the ambition which forces him finally to come to terms with the consequences of his actions. Even at the end he never enjoys the role he has. When Lady Macbeth dies, he says '*I have almost forgot the taste of fears*' (V, v, 9); this speech is not that of a man who enjoys the role of tyrant, but one who is aware of how much he as a man has changed. Indeed he even acknowledges to Macduff that '*my* *soul is too much charged with blood of thine already*' (V, viii, 5–6), which is close to a confession of guilt.

'*If th'assassination could trammel up the consequence*' (I, vii, 2–3), Macbeth wishes in his soliloquy before he kills Duncan. From being a soldier whose actions bring rewards, he has become a killer who must live with what he has done. The guilt his actions bring destroys him, as he knows it will. The fact that he acts despite that knowledge is what makes him a tragic hero.

Revision
(what you learn in this section)

- Macbeth is a brave warrior.
- Macbeth's ambition leads him on to become a hated tyrant.
- Macbeth is a man who thinks too much about his actions and the consequences of his actions.
- Evil is not a part of his nature, it is rather the consequence of his ambition. He never relishes the bloody role he plays.
- Despite being a bloody tyrant, he remains a fascinating character.

A few important quotes

Quote	Analysis
brave Macbeth *valiant cousin, worthy gentleman* *noble Macbeth* (I, ii, 16, 24, 67)	Others consider Macbeth to be a great and brave fighter.
Stars, hide your fires, *Let not light see my black and deep desires.* (I, iv, 50–51).	Macbeth is aware of his evil thoughts, and feels guilty about them.
too full o' the milk of human kindness (I, v, 16)	Lady Macbeth says this about him; it shows that she sees him as being weaker, softer and kinder than her.

what thou wouldst highly, *That wouldst thou holily.* (I, v, 19–20)	Lady Macbeth implies that he has ambition but wants to achieve every-thing in an honest fashion.
As his host, *Who should against his murderer shut the door,* *Not bear the knife myself.* (I, vii, 14–16)	Macbeth is aware of the evil he will be committing by killing Duncan.
Is this a dagger which I see before me, *The handle toward my hand?* (II, I, 33–34)	Macbeth is an imaginative person who sees things that others may not.
Sleep no more! *Macbeth does murder sleep.* (II, ii, 34–35)	Macbeth's conscience speaks to him, telling him he is a murderer.
To be thus is nothing, *But to be safely thus.* (III, i, 49–50)	To maintain his position, Macbeth feels the need to eliminate all his oppon-ents.
I am in blood *Stepped in so far that should I wade no more,* *Returning were as tedious as go o'er.* (III, iv, 136–138)	Macbeth says that once he has started killing, he may as well continue killing. His feelings are now immune to evil deeds.
tyrant *black Macbeth* (IV, iii, 36, 52)	Others have come to see Macbeth as a brutal and evil tyrant.

I have almost forgot the taste of fears; *The time has been, my senses would have cooled* *To hear a night-shriek, and my fell of hair* *Would at a dismal treatise rouse and stir* *As life were in't. I have supped full with horrors;* *Direness, familiar to my slaughterous thoughts,* *Cannot start me.* (V, v, 9–15)	knows what it means to have the normal feelings of a human being. Macbeth shows self-awareness: he realizes he has changed from a normal person into a tyrant who no longer

Lady Macbeth

Lady Macbeth has, over the years, come to be seen as an embodiment of evil: a fiendish creature who drives her weak husband to commit murder; an unnatural woman who says she would kill her own children if necessary; a monster. There is a connection between her and the evil as represented by the witches, as she takes on their **supernatural role**: '*Come, you spirits that tend on mortal thoughts, unsex me here*' (I, v, 39–40). Her desire to overthrow the natural order by rejecting her femininity would make her seem to the audience of the day as a more evil character than her husband; she is the '*fiend-like queen*' of the '*dead butcher*' (V, ix, 36). Moreover, her domination of her husband would have seemed like a reversal of the natural order for an audience of Shakespeare's time. For this reason the image of Lady Macbeth – despite her small role – as an evil character usually remains more impregnated in the minds of the audience than does her husband.

Yet it is also true, as critics have pointed out, that in her own world she can be seen as the **perfect wife**, supporting her husband in every way: strong when he is weak, loving when he needs comfort. It is she who advises him at the beginning and shows after her first piece of advice to '*look like the innocent flower, but be the serpent under't*' (I, v, 64–65) that she can actually follow this advice by her pretence of servility, loyalty and hospitality when Duncan arrives (I, vi).

The character of Lady Macbeth is problematic and every actor who plays the role has to decide how to portray her. Is she simply evil – a woman who will even sacrifice her own femininity in the cause of murder? Is she herself so hungry for power that she will do anything to make sure that her husband becomes king? Or does she know her husband so well – and love him so much – that she is there to support him and help him get what she knows he needs. Are both of these conflicting views equally correct?

It is not possible to understand Lady Macbeth without viewing her as a **partner to her husband**. She is so close to him that she may in fact be seen as one aspect of Macbeth's own personality. Yet her personality is not like that of Macbeth; it is only their thoughts which run along similar lines. As soon as she receives Macbeth's letter, telling her about the witches' prophecies, she immediately sees the implications, and without any of Macbeth's doubt and hesitation, she encourages him to kill the King. We have heard Macbeth's soliloquy and know he has similar thoughts, but she does not need to hear him voice them. She is already in step with him.

Examining the language of the play, we find many instances where their ideas mirror each other. Macbeth's '*Stars, hide your fires, let not light see my black and deep desires*' (I, iv, 50–51) is echoed by her '*Come, thick night, and pall thee in the dunnest smoke of hell*' (I, v, 49–50). Macbeth talks of '*the innocent sleep, sleep that knits up the ravelled sleave of care*' (II, ii, 35–36), and she tells him that he lacks '*the season of all natures, sleep*' (III, iv, 141).

Where Lady Macbeth differs from her husband is in her understanding of the consequences of her actions. She calls her husband a coward when he flinches from the murder and rebukes him when forgets to place the daggers beside the grooms, because she can see their actions only in terms of their results and not in terms of their consequences. Macbeth is a soldier. He knows how men react to scenes of blood and death. She does not have his experience. It seems, too, that all her energies are focused on action, not on imagination. She cannot imagine how she will feel. Early on, she does reveal a human side that had not been seen: her inability to kill Duncan as he '*resembled my father*' (II, ii, 12–13) puts all her cold-hearted speeches into perspective. Thus, when she fully understands the full horror of her actions and realizes a little water cannot wash the guilt away, she is driven mad and kills herself.

Yet it is hard to know much about Lady Macbeth because we do not see her except as a half of a couple (apart from her first appearance, when she is attached to Macbeth through his letter). She has no friend or confidante, and we know nothing about her except what she wants for her husband. She is a remarkably isolated character; everything about her is linked to her husband.

She is also a wife who knows her place in society. Duncan calls her '*our honoured hostess*' and '*fair and noble hostess*' (I, vi, 11 and 24). Even though she breaks the most fundamental rule of etiquette by having her guest and king murdered, she obeys the superficial rules of society. She worries that her husband does not give the correct toast at the right moment: '*you do not give the cheer*' (III, iv, 33). Without proper ceremony, she believes, it would be better to stay at home and eat there. Throughout this scene she tries her best to keep up the pretence to the nobles that everything is fine and make Macbeth remember that he has guests: '*My worthy lord, your noble friends do lack you*' (III, iv, 83–84). When it is clear that her husband is revealing himself, she destroys the social order by telling her guests to leave in as they like: '*Stand not upon the order of your going, but go at once*' (III, iv, 119–120). Society's laws no longer have any meaning for her; things cannot get any worse. She is destroyed, and after this scene we do not see her again until the sleep-walking scene in Act V, when we discover that her mind has deteriorated. It is this scene which allows Lady Macbeth to reveal her humanity. Her actions have pushed her into a private hell, and she will only find the sleep she so desires in death.

In many ways Lady Macbeth remains an enigma. Her behaviour when she urges her husband to kill is so removed from our own world that it is difficult to understand her. Yet she is not simply an embodiment of evil; when she finally realizes the consequences of her actions, she is destroyed. Moreover, there is no evidence of her personal ambition. She is ambitious for her husband, and apart from this, she has little knowledge of who she is. Therefore, to make Lady Macbeth a fully rounded character, it is necessary to interpret the clues from her language and behaviour. She is pragmatic as well as ruthless, courteous as well as deceitful, a loving wife who would kill her own child rather than go back once she has resolved to take action. Yet she has no understanding of the consequences that her actions will provoke. Unlike the witches, she cannot see into the future and is thus destroyed by the world she has created for herself.

Revision
(what you learn in this section)

- Lady Macbeth serves as a foil to Macbeth; one might even see them as being different sides of the same character.
- Lady Macbeth is a determined character who urges her husband to commit crimes to satisfy his own ambition.
- Lady Macbeth reinforces the theme of the reversal of the natural order by dominating her husband, by rejecting her gender, and by her willingness as a mother to kill her children if they stood in the way.
- Her cold-heartedness and rejection of her femininity make her more frightening that Macbeth.
- She is a strong character who fails to realize that her strength is no match for her conscience. Thinking about doing something is very different from doing it.

A few important quotes	
Quote	**Analysis**
Come, you spirits *That tend on mortal thought, unsex me here* *[…] make thick my blood* (I, v, 39–40, 42)	Lady Macbeth has a connection to the supernatural and wishes to destroy the natural order (here: her femininity).
look like the innocent flower, *But be the serpent under't.* (I, v, 64–65)	Lady Macbeth gives advice to her husband (here: to be two-faced)
our honoured hostess *fair and noble hostess* (I, vi, 11 and 24)	Duncan treats her as she appears to be: a noble and good lady.
Bring forth men-children only, *For thy undaunted mettle should compose* *Nothing but males.* (I, vii, 72–74)	Macbeth comments on the fact that his wife often seems more masculine than most men.
I shame *To wear a heart so white* (II, ii, 63–64)	She rebukes her husband for cowardice.
Out, damned spot! Out, I say! – One: two: why, then 'tis time to do't. – Hell is murky. – Fie, my lord, fie! A soldier, and afeard? What need we fear who knows it, when none can call our power account? – Yet who would have thought the old man to have had so much blood in him? (V, I, 33–38)	She becomes obsessed with the murders and cannot drive them out of her mind. Slowly she becomes mad.
fiend-like queen (V, ix, 36)	Others see Lady Macbeth as a devilish person.

Banquo

We first hear of Banquo in the wounded Sergeant's report (I, ii) as the captain who has fought fiercely by Macbeth's side. He arrives with Macbeth when they meet the Witches, and at this point he appears to be the hero's friend and confidant. He is dramatically necessary, so that Macbeth has someone with whom he can share his experiences. Yet this friendship is threatened even as it is introduced by Macbeth's reaction (I, iii, 84) to the witches' prediction that Banquo's sons will be kings, even though Banquo himself will not become king (I, iii, 65). It is Banquo who immediately reminds Macbeth of his own prophesied future: '*You shall be king*' (I, iii, 84). Already Macbeth has moved away from being the captain and Banquo's comrade, and seems set on founding a dynasty. Banquo has become a threat to Macbeth's security and peace of mind, and thus will become his second victim.

For Shakespeare, Banquo (a fictitious character) was actually the ancestor of King James. To please the King, Shakespeare therefore makes Banquo, in the witches' words, '*lesser than Macbeth and greater*' (I, iii, 63), not a king, but more importantly, the ancestor of a great line of kings.

Banquo's reaction to the witches is more rational and cautious than Macbeth's, as he warns him that the supernatural may well be deceptive: '*And oftentimes, to win us to our harm, the instruments of darkness tell us truths*' (I, iii, 122–123). Moreover, he is aware of the temptations offered by the witches' prophecies; this troubles him, but unlike Macbeth, he wishes to overcome the temptations: '*merciful powers, restrain in me the curséd thoughts that nature gives way to in repose*' (II, i, 7–9).

Despite his brief role in the play, Banquo's influence is strong. We are aware that it is he who, after Duncan's death, first suggests the need to '*question this most bloody piece of work*' (II, iii, 128). Here he also places himself on the side of good in a world increasingly infected by evil: '*In the great hand of God I stand*' (II, iii, 130). This follows his assertion that he would only accept honour if it was free of any dishonourable associations (II, i, 26-28). To Duncan he is '*noble Banquo*' (I, iv, 29) who is no less deserving of honours than Macbeth, and it is his '*royalty of nature*' (III, i, 51) that makes him a threat to Macbeth:

'*And to that dauntless temper of his mind, he hath a wisdom that doth guide his valour to act in safety*' (III, i, 53–55).

Banquo embodies Macbeth's conscience: '*Thou hast it now: king, Cawdor, Glamis, all, as the weird women promised, and, I fear, thou played'st most foully for't*' (III, i, 1-3). But with his dying words ('*Fly, good Fleance, fly, fly, fly*!', III, iii, 19) he ensures that his son will survive to become the first of that 'line of kings', the (Stuart) dynasty predicted by the Witches.

A few important quotes

Quote	Analysis
lesser than Macbeth and greater (I, iii, 63) *noble Banquo* *true, worthy Banquo* (I, iv, 29, 54) *right-valiant Banquo* (III, vi, 5). *royalty of nature* (III, i, 51) *And to that dauntless temper of his mind,* *He hath a wisdom that doth guide his valour* *To act in safety*' (III, i, 53–55)	These quotes serve to reinforce the idea that Banquo is a good man. This has less to do with his character (although, of course, the murder of a good man and friend like Banquo strengthens the feeling that Macbeth is evil) and more to do with the flattery of his descendant King James, hence 'greater' and 'royalty of nature', which serve to indicate that he is a worthy ancestor of kings.
merciful powers, *Restrain in me the cursèd thoughts that nature* *Gives way to in repose.* (II, i, 7–9)	Banquo actively fights against the temptations of the witches' prophecies; this shows him to be a person who prefers good to evil (unlike Macbeth).

Duncan

Duncan has a relatively small role in the play, but he has an important dramatic function. As the King, he is represented as a quasi-divine figure, the embodiment of wisdom and goodness. He personifies the strong masculine values of the fighter that are praised throughout the play: he honours Macbeth for his bloody fighting and orders Cawdor's execution for his treachery. But at the same time he appreciates natural beauty and has a gentle side: '*This castle hath a pleasant seat; the air nimbly and sweetly recommends itself unto our gentle senses*' (I, vi, 1–3). His appreciation of nature reflects the harmony of the natural order. Moreover, he is trusting: he believes in the natural loyalty of his subjects, but is betrayed – by the Thane of Cawdor as well as by Macbeth and his wife. Following his death, in contrast to Macbeth, he is portrayed as gracious, generous and humane. When Malcolm tests Macduff by pretending to be even more evil than Macbeth, Macduff reproaches him as one who blasphemes the memory of his father, '*a most sainted king*' (IV, iii, 109). '*Renown and grace is dead*' declares Macbeth (II, iii, 94), and however hypocritical this speech may be, it reinforces the image of Duncan as an ideal king, whose 'golden blood' has just been shed in the most unnatural manner. Duncan represents the ideal king, just as Macbeth represents the tyrant.

A few important quotes	
Quote	**Analysis**
Renown and grace is dead (II, iii, 94) *a most sainted king* (IV, iii, 109)	In a play about kingship, Duncan is described by others as a good king.

Malcolm

After the murder of his father, Malcolm is motivated by revenge, but also by the fact that the throne, promised to him by Duncan (I, iv, 37ff.), has been usurped. Even as he mourns his father and is distressed by the situation in Scotland, he is driven, above all, by his desire to reclaim the throne. What we know about him comes mostly from his own description: having pretended to Macduff that he was full of every vice, he then declares himself to be chaste, lacking in envy, and true to his word (IV, iii, 125–130). By thus testing Macduff's loyalty, he reveals himself to be a cautious politician. Equally, his skill as a general is shown when he orders that his army should not reveal its true numbers, but conceal itself behind cut branches (V, iv). At the end of the play, Malcolm prepares to be crowned king.

A few important quotes

Quote	Analysis
I am yet *Unknown to woman, never was forsworn,* *Scarcely have coveted what was mine own,* *At no time broke my faith, would not betray* *The devil to his fellow and delight* *No less in truth than life.* (IV, iii, 125–130)	In a play about kingship, Malcolm (like his father Duncan) encompasses the virtues a king should have.

Macduff

Macduff is introduced to the audience by the sound of loud knocking at the castle gate. The Elizabethan audience would recognise from earlier religious plays the sound of knocking as that of the dead knocking at the doors of Hell – an association reinforced by the words of the Porter. Macduff enters to the sound of fate knocking on the door, and from that moment, Macbeth's future is under threat.

Yet, to begin with, Macduff is hardly distinguished from the other thanes; he is the 'straight man' for the comic routine of the Porter, and though it is he who discovers Duncan's murder, it is Banquo who first begins to suspect Macbeth's guilt. Macduff's key dramatic function is revealed (in Act V) as the man who is '*not born of woman*' and who will therefore kill Macbeth. In the scene with Malcolm at the English court (IV, 3), he acts as a chorus, telling the audience of the tyranny that has engulfed Scotland: '*I think our country sinks beneath the yoke; it weeps, it bleeds*' (IV, iii, 39–40). These words are also a premonition of what Macduff will soon discover – the murder of his wife and children. Macduff's first response to this horrifying news is to blame himself. (His wife has said that Macduff's flight from Scotland, leaving her and her children unprotected, was 'madness'.) But his despair and tears are disdained by Malcolm, who wants him to display more masculine qualities: '*Dispute it like a man*' (IV, iii, 222). However, by the end of this scene Macduff has converted his pain into a desire for revenge. He becomes the fighter that Malcolm urges him to be, determined to be the one to kill Macbeth and allow the ghosts of his wife and children some peace. This ambition is realized and it is he who presents Macbeth's head to Malcolm and announces that Scotland is free (V, ix, 22).

The Porter

The Porter appears between Duncan's murder and the discovery of the crime (II, iii). While he provides the only comic relief in an otherwise relentless story of murder and brutality, he also provides a commentary on many of the themes of the play such as equivocation, damnation, ambition and treason.

Lady Macduff

Lady Macduff appears in only one scene, but her presence in the play is important for the contrast it shows between her normal emotions – her love for her children, her sense of betrayal, her belief in justice – and the abnormal cruelty of Lady Macbeth, who rejects any such feelings. In one of Shakespeare's most vivid scenes of unnecessary cruelty Lady Macduff and her young son (and other children offstage) are murdered, a deed that even Macbeth appears eventually to regret, since at the end of the play he tells Macduff he does not want to fight him, as his soul is already burdened with the blood of his family (V, viii, 5–6).

Ross

Ross's main function in the play is that of a messenger, informing Macbeth that he is now Thane of Cawdor and bringing Macduff the report of the murder of his wife and children. He also tries to warn Lady Macduff of the danger she is in, but does not stay to defend her. In fact, he seems to the kind of person who survives by making sure he is on the winning side, staying with Macbeth until he sees more advantage in joining Malcolm and Macduff.

Lennox

Lennox, like Ross, is a survivor, who stays with Macbeth until he has the opportunity to change sides. He also has the function of a chorus in his scene with the Lord (III, vi), summarizing the events that have taken place and bringing the audience up to date. We also see in this scene that, like Ross, he is cautious about declaring his true beliefs.

Siward

Siward is a professional soldier, a tough military character, whose main concern on learning of the death of his son is whether Young Siward has died a proper soldier's death. This allows Malcolm to rebuke him for not feeling more of a loss, and suggests that there may have been some change in Malcolm since his refusal to allow Macduff to show his feelings on receiving the news of the murder of his family. (This could equally be seen as an inconsistency in Malcolm's character.)

The Old Man and the Lord

These are two nameless characters who have the function of a chorus, giving the audience information and commenting on the action. Interestingly, they are at opposite ends of the social scale, giving an impression of how the events are affecting the whole country, from the royal court to the ordinary people.

The Doctor

The Doctor is called in to diagnose Lady Macbeth's condition. He understands the significance of her semi-conscious confessions, but '*dare not speak*'. He reflects the fear of people living under a tyrant's regime, and also develops the imagery of sickness and healing that runs through the play. When Macbeth asks if he can cure his wife, he replies in a way that will be familiar to a modern audience: '*Therein the patient must minister to himself*' (V, iii, 46–47).

The Witches

The witches in Macbeth should not be regarded as true characters but rather more representatives of evil; they have three basic functions. Their plot function is to plant in Macbeth's mind the idea which results in all the subsequent action; they move the drama forward. They also function to demonstrate the essential nature of Macbeth's character: when he returns to them (IV, i), he shows that he is on the side of evil. And, from the very beginning, they establish the atmosphere of the play. '*Fair is foul and foul is fair*' (I, i, 12), they chant, announcing to the audience that the values of the world they are entering are reversed, and this line resonates throughout the play. '*Peace, the charm's wound up*' (I, iii, 35), they declare as Macbeth and Banquo enter for the first time, but it is not only the characters who will be bound up in this charm; so will the audience, as they are drawn into the dark action of the play. '*So foul and fair a day I have not seen*' (1, iii, 36), Macbeth announces, his very first words echoing those of the witches, and while they may mean something very different – he may be reflecting on the battle and its outcome – they tell the audience that he is connected in some way to the supernatural world of witchcraft. Our first experience of Macbeth, therefore, is that of '*the selfsame tune and words*' (I, iii, 86) as the witches, so it should not surprise us that he wishes to spend more time with them: '*Would they had stayed*' (I, iii, 80). It is Banquo who wonders if they are hallucinating: '*Or have we eaten on the insane root that takes the reason prisoner?*' (1, iii, 82–83). Macbeth is already gripped by their magical promises of kingship.

The word 'witch' is mentioned only once in the text, when the First Witch recalls an insult against herself. To Banquo, they are '*instruments of darkness*' (I, iii, 123), to Lady Macbeth '*metaphysical aid*' (I, v, 28) and to Macbeth the '*weird sisters*' (III, iv, 133) and '*secret, black and midnight hags*' (IV, i, 48). It is clear that Shakespeare intended them to be forces of evil and wanted his audience to fear them. They are linked with the images of darkness that fill the play – and it is worth noting (see

'Darkness', p. 72) that the word 'fear' appears more often in *Macbeth* than in any other Shakespeare play.

Revision
(what you learn about the minor characters)

- The minor characters are not round characters. Rather they represent ideals and status. Duncan and Malcolm throw light on what a king should be like (i.e. the opposite of Macbeth). The witches represent supernatural evil. Macduff symbolizes revenge and Macbeth's fate.

Vocabulary

Here are some vocabulary items that you can use when talking about the characters.

Macbeth courageous warrior/fighter ambitious, ruthless, murderous, despicable, tyrannical, brutal, disloyal subject, tyrant, usurper obedient husband, easily influenced, weak-willed, remorseful, fearful, hypocritical, two-faced ambition is his tragic flaw / fatal weakness he has finer feelings / a sensitive/reflective character his manhood is important to him
Lady Macbeth domineering, scheming, cunning, unscrupulous, masculine, determined, resolute, persuasive, practical, haunted, evil, unpleasant rejects her femininity driven crazy by guilt
Duncan an ideal king, strong leader, just ruler saintly, regal, trusting, gentle, fair
Banquo courageous, regal, wise, perceptive, trusting

Themes

Good/Evil

Macbeth is a play full of antitheses, of pairs of opposing themes. The opening scene, which can be seen to function as a prologue, announces the central opposition – between good and evil. This theme is represented in the play on a personal level by Macbeth's struggle with his conscience, and on a broader, political level, by the contrast between Duncan's absolute virtue and Macbeth's limitless capacity for evil.

The play unfolds in a world turned upside down, where '*Fair is foul, and foul is fair*' (I, i, 12), a world under the influence of dark, supernatural forces, where good and evil are utterly confused. When Macbeth first meets the witches, he observes that '*This supernatural soliciting cannot be ill, cannot be good*' (I, iii, 129–139); and when Lady Macduff is advised to escape, she reflects, '*I am in this earthly world where to do harm is often laudable, to do good sometime accounted dangerous folly*' (IV, ii, 73–75). Even Malcolm, who seems by the end of the play to have inherited at least some of his father's virtuous qualities, has to pretend to be capable of greater evil than Macbeth, in order to test Macduff's loyalty (IV, iii). After the death of Duncan, goodness is largely absent, either destroyed (in the brutal murders of Banquo and Macduff's family) or in retreat (in the flight of Fleance and Duncan's sons). The audience only witnesses the killing of characters close to Macbeth, but various reports (III, vi; IV, iii; V, ii) about the worsening situation in Scotland suggest that the whole country is suffering under Macbeth's despotic rule. By contrast, the English King Edward is presented as a figure of supreme goodness, able with his touch to cure a disease called 'the Evil'. Ultimately, goodness triumphs over evil, and the play, which begins with the demonic evil of the witches, concludes with Malcolm promising to do good in the name of God ('*by the grace of Grace*', V, ix, 39).

Order/Disorder

The need for order was a fundamental idea in the Elizabethan view of the world. It was believed that everyone had a fixed place in a 'Great Chain of Being', which extended from God right down to the lowest forms of life. In this world picture, the King or Queen was seen as divinely appointed, placed just below the angels. Thus, the killing of a king was the worst imaginable crime. The need to preserve this natural order is a frequent theme in Shakespeare's plays (cf. *Julius Caesar*, *Hamlet*, *King Lear*, *Richard II*, *Richard III*), and throughout *Macbeth* we see how the murder of Duncan produces total disorder. Not only is the social order disrupted, but nature itself becomes chaotic, as the day turns dark and animals behave unnaturally (II, iv, 4–20).

The political action of the play begins with Duncan's defeat of the rebels and the restoration of order, but this apparent harmony has already been undermined in the opening scene by the witches, who have announced their intention to meet Macbeth and who will instigate his transformation from an agent of order into its destroyer. Later on, Macbeth's coronation banquet, which should be the most formal celebration of order, becomes instead a symbol of the breakdown of the natural order (III, iv, 109–110, 119–120). Disorder is also a synonym for sickness, and Scotland itself is personified as a body that can only be restored to health when Duncan's legitimate heir is restored to the throne. The invitation to his coronation is Malcolm's first action after the death of Macbeth, and the last word in the play, 'Scone', is the sacred throne of the kings of Scotland.

Crime/Punishment

The conflicts of good/evil and order/disorder are paralleled by the opposition that runs through the play between crime and punishment. In a world where the king has absolute, God-given authority, rebellion is regarded as sacrilege and is automatically punishable by death. In his final moments, the Thane of Cawdor expresses '*deep repentance*', accepting the justice of his punishment and begging for the King's forgiveness (I, iv, 5–8). When Macbeth first thinks of the possibility of murdering Duncan, he rejects the idea in horror and hopes that 'chance' might crown him (I, iii, 130–143). But once Duncan has named Malcolm as his successor, Macbeth begins to realize that the most terrible of crimes will be the only way he can fulfil the witches' prophecy (I, iv, 48–53). He almost abandons the plan to kill the King, tormented by thoughts of judgement and retribution, in the next world as well as on Earth (I, vii, 1–28). By contrast, Lady Macbeth refuses to think about such consequences ('*If we should fail?*' / '*We fail!*'; I, vii, 59).

Once the worst crime has been committed, however, Macbeth finds it easier to order the murders of Banquo and Fleance, though Banquo's ghost reminds him of the probability of punishment ('*blood will have blood*'; III, iv, 122). As Macbeth says '*I am in blood stepped in so far that, should I wade no more, returning were as tedious as go o'er*' (III, iv, 136–137). But reassured by his second meeting with the witches, Macbeth orders the killing of Macduff's family without any hesitation (IV, i, 145–157). In the final act, Macbeth has no thought of punishment – only an animal instinct for survival – until the ultimate punishment is delivered by Macduff. His act of regicide has put him outside the reach of God's grace, so he becomes no longer fully human.

Appearance/Reality

Throughout the play, appearances are constantly deceptive. Duncan has already been betrayed by Cawdor, '*a gentleman on whom I built an absolute trust*' (I, iv, 13–14) and he is fatally deceived by Macbeth's apparent loyalty and hospitality. His praise of the surroundings of Macbeth's castle (I, vi, 1–3) indicates to the audience how he has misinterpreted the situation. However, it is not entirely his fault, as Macbeth is hiding his disloyalty, as his wife urges him to '*look like the innocent flower, but be the serpent under't*' (I, v, 64–65). This strategy is also employed by Malcolm, but exactly the other way round, in order to test Macduff's loyalty (IV, iii).

After Duncan's death, Macbeth tries at first to maintain the outward appearance of a legitimate ruler, but as his crimes multiply, those around him recognize the reality and eventually desert him.

The supernatural elements in the play also reinforce the theme of appearance versus reality. The witches mislead Macbeth with prophecies that appear to offer him security, but which in reality turn out to be tricks. Banquo at first thinks that the witches are hallucinations and their promises false ('*Were such things here as we do speak about? Or have we eaten on the insane root that takes the reason prisoner?*'; I, iii, 81–83), though later he is tempted to believe in their reality ('*If there come truth from them – as upon thee, Macbeth, their speeches shine*'; III, i, 6–7). Macbeth's visions of the dagger and Banquo's ghost, appear to him but to no one else, and they may be seen as projections of his repressed guilt. When in the final act he realizes the truth about Macduff's birth, his eyes are finally opened: '*And be these juggling fiends no more believed that palter with us in a double sense*' (V, viii, 19–20).

He seems at first to be conscious of how unreliable appearances may be ('*nothing is, but what is not*'; I, iii, 140–141), but is soon prepared to deceive himself ('*[Let not] the eye wink at the hand. Yet let that be, which the eye fears, when it is done, to see*'; I, iv, 52–53).

Naturalness/Unnaturalness

Macbeth, pretending to be horrified by the discovery of Duncan's murder, describes the stab wounds in the King's flesh as '*a breach in nature*' (II, iii, 113). This image provides a key to one of the principal themes in Macbeth – the ways in which the natural order of the world is upset by unnatural actions ('*unnatural deeds do breed unnatural troubles*'; V, i, 66–67). 'Nature' is one of the most frequently used words in the play, referring not only to the natural world of weather, animals and plants, but also to the normal personalities of individual characters and to their moral behaviour. All these forms of nature are transformed into their unnatural opposites by the greatest crime against nature – regicide.

Yet before the regicide takes place, the forces of the supernatural start the process in motion. Macbeth, unsure whether the witches are good or evil, recognises them as '*supernatural*' (I, iii, 129), which suggests forces that are unnatural rather than 'more than natural'.

Just before Macbeth kills the King, nature already '*seems dead*', and he appeals to the earth itself not to hear his footsteps (II, i, 50–60); after the murder, Duncan's horses turn '*wild in nature*' as if they are at '*war with mankind*' (II, iv, 16–18); and when Macbeth returns to the witches, he is prepared to risk the destruction of the entire natural world for the answers he wants from them ('*though the treasure of nature's germens tumble all together, even till destruction sicken*'; IV, i, 58–60). Lady Macbeth calls on spirits to 'unsex' her and make her unnaturally cruel (I, v, 39–49); eventually she cannot achieve the natural peace of sleep – '*great Nature's second course*' (II, ii, 38) – and her sleepwalking is described by the doctor as '*a great perturbation in nature*' (V, i, 9). When Macbeth first thinks of murder, the idea seems '*against the use of nature*' (I, iii, 136) and his wife fears that his nature is '*too full o' the milk of human kindness*' (I, v, 16). The different meanings of 'nature' can also be seen in relation to Banquo: Macbeth fears his '*royalty of nature*' (III, i, 51); Banquo himself resists '*the cursèd thoughts that nature gives way to in repose*' (II, i, 8–9); and finally, the murderers report that the least of Banquo's wounds is '*a death to nature*' (III, iv, 28). But it is Macduff who best sums up the unnaturalness of Macbeth's unlimited excesses: '*Boundless intemperance in nature is a tyranny*' (IV, iii, 66–67).

Ambition

Ambition can be a positive human quality, but in *Macbeth* we see the destructive effects of ambition when it is corrupted. Lady Macbeth, learning of the witches' prophecies, acknowledges that her husband is '*not without ambition*' (I, v, 18). By his own admission, Macbeth is driven by '*vaulting ambition which o'erleaps itself*' (I, vii, 27), but in the past his ambition has been limited by a basic sense of right and wrong, and Lady Macbeth fears that he may not possess '*the illness [that] should attend it*' (I, v, 19), i.e. ruthlessness. When Macbeth receives the news that he has been named Earl of Cawdor, he expects Banquo to be equally ambitious (I, iii, 117–119), while his wife recognizes the contradiction hinted at in his letter: '*what thou wouldst highly, that wouldst thou holily; wouldst not play false, and yet wouldst wrongly win*' (I, v, 19–21). Her own ambitious instincts are totally untroubled by any such reservations, and she is determined to urge him on. She realizes that he is wavering, wanting to pursue his ambitions but afraid to follow through on the logic of what needs to be done to get the crown. The crown, as well as being an emblem of kingship, functions in the play as a symbol of Macbeth's ambition, and when, without any hesitation, he orders the killing of Macduff's family, the decision is made '*to crown my thoughts with acts*' (IV, 1, 150). By this point in the play, his determination to hold on to the throne (reinforced by the use of 'crown' as a verb) allows him none of his earlier moral doubts. Only when he is isolated in his castle and awaiting the arrival Malcolm's army does Macbeth reflect on the results of his 'vaulting ambition': '*And that which should accompany old age, as honour, love, obedience, troops of friends, I must not look to have*' (V, iii, 24–26).

Violence/Tyranny

Tyranny is always achieved and sustained through violence, and *Macbeth* is one of Shakespeare's most violent plays. Although most of the killings take place off stage, they are reported in such graphic detail, often by characters with blood on their hands, that we almost feel we have witnessed them. The play is framed by two bloody battles: in the first Macbeth savagely slaughters Macdonald, while in the second he is beheaded by Macduff. Between these two legitimate killings, there is the sequence of murders – of Duncan and his grooms, Banquo, Lady Macduff and her son – committed or ordered by Macbeth. One contemporary critic has suggested that the play is not simply the story of a good and righteous king usurped by an illegitimate tyrant, but that the key distinction is between authorized, 'state-sponsored' violence and crime committed for purely personal advancement.

Almost as soon as he takes over the throne, Macbeth becomes known as the '*tyrant*' (III, vi, 22). Not only is he responsible for the murders shown in the play, but it becomes apparent that the whole country is suffering under his brutal rule: '*each new morn, new widows howl, new orphans cry, new sorrows strike heaven on the face*' (IV, iii, 4–6). Scotland '*sinks beneath the yoke; it weeps, it bleeds, and each new day a gash is added to her wounds*' (IV, iii, 39–41). Macbeth is portrayed as stabbing Scotland, just as he has stabbed the King.

When he tests Macduff's loyalty, Malcolm provides a clear contrast between the nature of a king and that of a tyrant, pretending that he lacks '*the king-becoming graces – as justice, verity, temperance, stableness, bounty, perseverance, mercy, lowliness, devotion, patience, courage, fortitude*' (IV, iii, 92–94), and claiming that, like Macbeth, he will be '*bloody, luxurious, avaricious, false, deceitful, sudden, malicious, smacking of every sin that has a name*' (IV, iii, 57–60). The legitimate king is the personification of virtue and justice, whereas the tyrant is a 'devilish' man, as a result of whose actions Scotland 'weeps' and 'bleeds'.

Guilt/Conscience

The guilt felt by Macbeth, and to a far lesser extent by Lady Macbeth, is what makes their characters interesting and also the source of much of the play's dramatic tension. Before the murder of Duncan, Macbeth's conscience almost prevents him from taking action, and it is only his wife's relentless provocation that drives him on. Immediately after the murder, he is struck by the enormity of his crime, believing he has heard a voice crying out: '*Macbeth shall sleep no more*' (II, ii, 42). (And after the banquet, we learn that he is indeed unable to sleep: '*You lack the season of all natures, sleep*'; III, iv, 141.) He is unable to say 'Amen' when he overhears the grooms' prayers and refuses to return to them: '*I am afraid to think what I have done*' (II, ii, 50).

The more murders he commits, the less Macbeth is troubled by feelings of guilt, though the appearance of Banquo's ghost (which unlike the witches is visible only to him) is a clear indication of his troubled conscience. And towards the end Angus suggests that Macbeth's reported madness is caused by his growing feelings of guilt, '*Now does he feel his secret murders sticking on his hands*' (V, ii, 16–17).

Lady Macbeth is, on the other hand, initially scornful of this weakness and feels no guilt whatsoever; when she faints at the news of the murder, it is not clear whether this is a sign of a sudden attack of nerves or a trick to mislead the thanes. However, while Macbeth almost comes to accept with his guilt and wickedness, Lady Macbeth is eventually overwhelmed by guilt, so that she is driven insane. Finally she expresses her own guilt in the sleepwalking scene, though it is worth noting that she is only able to make this confession in her sleep. In the closing speech of the play, Malcolm reports that her death may have been suicide, but again we do not know whether this was the result of a guilty conscience or an act of desperation in the face of imminent capture and probable execution.

Shakespeare's emphasis on Macbeth's conscience would have pleased King James, who had written extensively about the role of conscience in *Basilicon Doron* (1598), a book designed to teach his young son the morality of kingship.

Destiny/Free will

England in the early 17th century was still influenced by the superstitions of the Middle Ages with widespread belief in witches and prophecies. The idea of supernatural forces controlling human lives is established in the opening scene of *Macbeth*, but subsequent events are really the result of purely human agency. The witches' prophecies and

Macbeth's reactions to them create the conflict in the play between destiny and free will. If Macbeth believed only in his own ability to shape his destiny or if he took the prophecies at face value and waited for '*chance*' to crown him (I, iii, 143), the play would have no dramatic tension. Macbeth is the tragedy of a man poised uneasily between ancient superstition and a new spirit of self-belief. The first report we hear of him is of a warrior '*disdaining fortune*' (I, ii, 17), but this rational, practical soldier is shaken by the fulfilment of the first prophecy ('*My thought […] shakes so my single state of man that function is smothered in surmise*'; I, iii, 138–140). Lady Macbeth seems to have a far more straightforward belief in '*fate and metaphysical aid*' (I, v, 28), but the choices that she and her husband make are their own, and the witches' prophecies can be seen as coming at the moment when they were ready to hear them. Macbeth is told he will become King, but he is not told how, and it is his freely made choices, rather than unalterable destiny, that are responsible for his ultimate downfall.

Manliness

The concept of manliness is questioned throughout the play. The conventional view of manliness as physical courage is expressed by Lennox, when he reports that the English forces include '*many unrough youths that even now protest their first of manhood*' (V, ii, 10-11), and by Ross, describing Young Siward as dying '*like a man*' (V, ix, 9), while Siward himself is content that his son died with his wounds 'on the front' (V, ix, 13). This traditional concept of manliness as bravery in battle is only briefly questioned by Malcolm (V, ix, 17–18), but his view is rejected by Siward.

Ironically, the murderers, too, when challenged by Macbeth, define themselves in the same terms: '*We are men, my liege*' (III, i, 94).

The idea of manly behaviour is called into question when Macduff receives the news of the murder of his wife and children: Malcolm wants him to '*dispute it like a man*' and take his revenge, but Macduff insists that first he must '*feel it as a man*' (IV, iii, 222–223). At this moment of sudden bereavement, Macduff sees grief as more 'manly' than bloody revenge. However, just a few lines later, Macduff no longer wants to '*play the woman*' (IV, iii, 232) and is ready for revenge, which Malcolm applauds: '*This tune goes manly*' (IV, iii, 237).

But the most intensive debate about manliness occurs between Lady Macbeth and Macbeth. When she reproaches him for wanting to abandon their plan to murder Duncan, he protests: '*I dare do all that may become a man*' (I, vii, 46). But for her it is the murder that will prove his manliness, and she challenges him further by renouncing womanly qualities and assuring him that she would murder her own child if she had sworn to do so. Macbeth is persuaded, and suggests that she should '*Bring forth men-children only*' (I, vii, 72). When Macbeth breaks down at the banquet, Lady Macbeth accuses him of being '*quite unmanned in folly*' (III, iv, 73), and asks '*Are you a man?*' (III, iv, 58), deriding his fears as '*impostors to true fear, [that] would well become a woman's story at a winter's fire*' (III, iv, 64–65). Again, she succeeds in provoking Macbeth, and he confronts the ghost of Banquo, boasting '*What man dare, I dare*' (III, iv, 99). While Lady Macbeth exults in her 'manly' nature (which is unnatural), Macbeth's manliness is never really resolved. By the end of the play manliness belongs to Malcolm and his invading army, and Macbeth is reduced to the level of an animal, like a bear tied to a stake: '*bear-like, I must fight the course*' (V, vii, 2). So one may say that a certain degree of upright behaviour is essential to be comfortable with one's manliness.

Equivocation

Equivocation – telling a half-truth so as to avoid actually lying – was a notion that had captured the public's imagination at the time that *Macbeth* was written. Henry Garnet, leader of the English Jesuits from 1587, was tried and executed in 1606 (the probable date of *Macbeth's* first performance) for his involvement in the previous year's Gunpowder Plot to blow up Parliament (cf. p. 8). Garnet had written *A Treatise on Equivocation*, recommending Catholics to hide their religious faith, as God would know the whole truth. Garnet himself had at first equivocated in an attempt to conceal his knowledge of the conspiracy. The Porter, imagining himself to be the gatekeeper to Hell, welcomes a series of sinners, including '*an equivocator that could swear in both the scales against either scale*' (II, iii, 9–10). He also jokes that alcohol is an equivocator, arousing sexual appetite, but then leading to disappointment.

More seriously, equivocation has already been identified with the witches, when Banquo suspects that '*oftentimes, to win us to our harm, the instruments of darkness tell us truths; win us with honest trifles, to betray's in deepest consequence*' (I, iii, 122–125). Even their language is full of antithesis: '*When the battle's lost, and won*' (I, i, 4), '*Fair is foul, and foul is fair*' (I, i, 12), '*Lesser than Macbeth, and greater*' (I, iii, 63). The most damaging equivocations in the play are the deceptive reassurances Macbeth receives when he visits the witches. By the time he realizes how he has been misled ('*be these juggling fiends no more believed that palter with us in a double sense*'; V, viii, 19–20; and '*I … begin to doubt the equivocation of the fiend that lies like truth*'; V, v, 41–43), when Birnam Wood has '*come*' to Dunsinane and he has met the man who is not '*of woman born*', it is too late.

Language and Style

Imagery

Darkness/Light

From the opening of the play, when the audience meets the '*secret, black and midnight hags*' (IV, i, 48), we are taken into a world filled with darkness, where '*fair is foul, and foul is fair*' (I, i, 12). The witches are, in Banquo's words, '*the instruments of darkness*' (I, iii, 123) and images of darkness fill the play. Macbeth invokes the power of the night to conceal his deeds: '*Stars, hide your fires, let not light see my black and deep desires*' (I, iv, 50–51), a wish echoed by his wife: '*Come, thick night, and pall thee in the dunnest smoke of hell, that my keen knife see not the wound it makes*' (I, v, 49–51). Macbeth repeats this wish before the murder of Banquo, imploring the night to '*Scarf up the tender eye of pitiful day*' while '*night's black agents to their preys do rouse*' (III, ii, 47, 52). The result of the unnatural murder committed by Macbeth has even made day become night, as Ross comments: '*'tis day, and yet dark night strangles the travelling lamp. […] Darkness does the face of earth entomb*' (II, iv, 7–9). Macbeth has not only '*murdered sleep*'; he has transformed nature. His world has become so dark that when Lady Macbeth appears in the sleepwalking scene, she is carrying a taper with her because she has ordered that '*she has light by her continually*' (V, i, 21–22). When Macbeth hears of her death, he uses the image of a light for life itself: '*Out, out, brief candle*' (V, v, 21–22), echoing the words of Banquo at the time of Duncan's murder: '*There's husbandry in heaven, their candles are all out*' (II, i, 4–5). By his actions, Macbeth has extinguished all natural light and created a world of perpetual darkness.

Blood

From the outset, Macbeth is filled with powerful images of bloodshed, and blood is mentioned numerous times in the play. The play starts and ends with a bloody battle. In Act I, Scene 2, a '*bleeding captain*' describes the carnage of battle where Macbeth wields a sword '*which smoked with bloody execution*' (I, ii, 18). Macbeth is described as killing Macdonald by cutting him from the navel to the jaw.

But blood, which it is honourable to spill in battle, soon becomes the '*bloody business*' (II, i, 48) of killing Duncan. This act is so unnatural that Duncan's royal blood is seen to be unlike that of other men; it is golden: '*If he do bleed, I'll gild the faces of the grooms*' (II, ii, 54–55), '*his silver skin laced with his golden blood*' (II, iii, 112).

Both Lady Macbeth and her husband are seen to have bloody hands after the murder, but while Macbeth feels contaminated ('*Will all great Neptune's ocean wash this blood clean from my hand?*'; II, ii, 59–60), Lady Macbeth taunts him that such a feeling is cowardly: '*My hands are of your colour; but I shame to wear a heart so white*' (II, ii, 63–64). Yet she will echo his feelings precisely by the end of the play when she sleepwalks: '*Yet who would have thought the old man to have had so much blood in him?*' (V, i, 36–38), '*Here's the smell of the blood still; all the perfumes of Arabia will not sweeten this little hand*' (V, i, 47–48).

Macbeth's reign has become that of '*an untitled tyrant, bloody-sceptred*' (IV, iii, 104) and the earth itself a '*bloody stage*' (II, iv, 6). Killing becomes an act that requires more killing ('*It will have blood, they say; blood will have blood*'; III, iv, 122), until Macbeth realizes with a kind of exhaustion that his only solution is to continue to kill: '*I am in blood stepped in so far that should I wade no more, returning were as tedious as go o'er*' (III, iv, 136–138).

Sleep

Sleep is a powerful image in Macbeth, and the play contains some of the most powerful and beautiful images of sleep in the English language: '*Sleep that knits up the ravelled sleave of care, the death of each day's care, sore labour's bath, balm of hurt minds, great Nature's second course, chief nourisher in life's feast*' (II, ii, 36–39). Its positive and life-giving qualities are contrasted with the absence of sleep, which is connected with a guilty conscience. Macbeth kills Duncan while he is sleeping and implicates the sleeping grooms, but while the dead Duncan now '*sleeps well*' after '*life's fitful fever*' (III, ii, 23), Macbeth believes that he can hear a voice that makes sleep itself the victim of his crime: '*Methought I heard a voice cry, "Sleep no more! Macbeth does murder sleep"*' (II, ii, 34–35). This delusion echoes the curse that one of the witches placed on the sailor whose wife had insulted her: '*I'll drain him dry as hay: sleep shall neither night nor day hang upon his penthouse lid;*

he shall live a man forbid' (I, iii, 17–20). The actions taken by Macbeth have caused him to have nightmares that prevent him from sleeping. This is seen by his wife as the reason for his hallucinations and his strange behaviour: '*You lack the season of all natures, sleep*' (III, iv, 141). Her lack of conscience, by comparison, allows her to sleep until she finally becomes aware of the consequences of their actions. However, it is during her sleep that her guilt haunts her, so she takes to sleepwalking.

Sleep in the play is also seen to imitate death. When Macduff calls Malcolm and Donalbain to see their father's corpse, he tells them to '*Shake off this downy sleep, death's counterfeit, and look on death itself*' (II, iii, 77–78). Lady Macbeth tells her husband that '*the sleeping and the dead are but as pictures*' (II, ii, 52–53). The connection between sleep and death continues through the play until her own passage from sleepwalking to death.

Clothes

The image of ill-fitting or unsuitable clothing is frequently used in the play to symbolize Macbeth's unsuitability as a king. When Macbeth is first hailed as Thane of Cawdor, after Cawdor has been sentenced to death, he answers: '*The Thane of Cawdor lives. Why do you dress me in borrowed robes?*' (I, iii, 106–107). He is seen here as a soldier who does not adapt easily to new honours. Banquo, mistaking Macbeth's thoughtfulness as unease at his new title (whereas he is actually already thinking ahead to murder) comments that: '*New honours come upon him like our strange garments, cleave not to their mould but with the aid of use*' (I, iii, 144–146). As Ross leaves for Macbeth's coronation, Macduff also uses the metaphor of clothing, referring to the past in terms of attire: '*Lest our old robes sit easier than our new*' (II, iv, 38). When Macbeth hesitates over killing Duncan, he again uses the imagery of clothing to describe how he would like to enjoy his good reputation: '*I have bought golden opinions from all sorts of people, which would be worn now in their newest gloss, not cast aside so soon*' (I, vii, 32–35). Lady Macbeth takes up the same image: '*Was the hope drunk wherein you dressed yourself?*' (I, vii, 35–36). It is in his armour that he feels most secure – as a soldier, he was not responsible for the consequence of his actions. But these actions have now brought him a crown, and this does not fit so well. As

Angus observes, Macbeth now feels '*his title hang loose about him, like a giant's robe upon a dwarfish thief*' (V, ii, 20–22).

Disease and Medicine

The world of *Macbeth* is infected with sickness and disease, and images of health and illness are used to reinforce the theme of order and disorder. The first scene with the witches introduces us to a world of pestilence with its '*fog and filthy air*' (I, i, 13).

The sickness in the play is mostly concerned with mental disorder. Inability to sleep afflicts Macbeth, conscience-stricken after Duncan's murder, and his wife sees this as a sign of mental sickness, '*You do unbend your noble strength to think so brain-sickly of things*' (II, ii, 44–45). Lady Macbeth explains away her husband's strange behaviour at the banquet by claiming that he has suffered from such 'fits' since his youth. When she reappears in the final act, it is she whose sleep is troubled. When the Doctor tells Macbeth that he is unable to heal her '*infected*' mind and the patient must cure herself, Macbeth curses medicine, exclaiming '*Throw physic to the dogs. I'll none of it.*' (V, iii, 48).

Macbeth tells the murderers he will remain '*sickly*' while Banquo lives, but that Banquo's death will restore him to '*perfect*' health (III, i). And when Macbeth demands answers from the witches at the risk of universal death and destruction, he goes even further and imagines destruction itself growing sick (IV, i, 60). Finally, with his wife demented and most of his followers gone, Macbeth tells Seyton that he is '*sick at heart*' (V, iii, 19).

The sickness of Macbeth and Lady Macbeth is in sharp contrast to the curative powers of the saintly King Edward, whose '*healing benediction*' is able to cure the victims of scrofula, said by Malcolm to be the '*despair of surgery*' (IV, iii, 158, 154).

Disease also becomes a metaphor for everything that is wrong in Scotland. The country is described as a diseased patient by Ross (IV, iii, 166–175) and by Caithness (V, ii, 27–29), and the '*medicine of the sickly weal*' is Malcolm, the rightful king. We sense Macbeth's imminent defeat when he uses the same image, wishing that the Doctor could cure the sickness in Scotland, but here he feels the sickness is the English army (V, iii, 51–57).

Animals

The first reference to an animal in the play is by the witches to their 'familiars' – a cat 'Graymalkin' and a toad, 'Paddock'. Association with such 'familiar spirits' or demons, which were said to take the form of pet animals, was one of the defining characteristics of English witches. The familiars were said to suck blood from a special nipple hidden somewhere on the witch's body, and witch hunters looked for this as a sign of witchcraft. Shakespeare's audience would have known which animals were associated with the supernatural, and the play demonstrates a clear distinction between animals with positive qualities and creatures traditionally associated with evil – animals such as rats and toads, and dark birds such as crows and ravens. The First Witch compares herself to '*a rat without a tail*' (I, iii, 8); Macbeth describes the oncoming night: '*Light thickens; and the crow makes wing to the rooky wood*' (III, ii, 49–50); and Lady Macbeth announces: '*The raven himself is hoarse that croaks the fatal entrance of Duncan under my battlements*' (I, v, 37–39). One of the witches' actions, in fact, is killing (good) farm animals: '*Where hast thou been, sister?*' '*Killing swine*' (I, iii, 1–2). In Act IV, Scene 1 the witches list the animals they have used in their potion, all of which represent in some way evil or unpleasantness.

Macbeth and Banquo, by contrast, are in their bravery on the battlefield compared to positive animals: like eagles killing sparrows or lions killing hares (I, ii, 35). The Third Apparition tells Macbeth to be '*lion-mettled*' (IV, i, 91), but by the end of the play his bravery has deserted him and he is reduced to the level of a bear to be baited (an activity known to have taken place near the Globe Theatre): '*bear-like, I must fight the course*' (V, vii, 2).

Babies/Children

'*He has no children!*' shouts Macduff in despair after he hears that his wife and children have been slaughtered (IV, iii, 218), and it is not surprising that Sigmund Freud found *Macbeth* to be full of references to father–child relationships. The murder of Duncan, he argued, could be read as a son killing his father, though it is Duncan's resemblance to Lady Macbeth's father that prevents her from killing him (II, ii, 12–13).

Babies and children form a powerful thread of imagery that runs through the play. It is the thought of Banquo's children becoming future kings that drives Macbeth to kill Banquo, though his son does escape. In order to ensure the continuation of his dynasty, Macbeth is willing to commit the most terrible crime and murder children. The unnaturalness of this action is emphasized at various points in the play. The witches use the finger of a '*birth-strangled babe*' (IV, i, 30) in their spells, and a bloody child followed by a crowned one are shown to Macbeth in the apparition scene. Macbeth describes pity as a '*naked new-born babe*' (I, vii, 21) but Lady Macbeth shows herself to be quite pitiless by replying that while she has known the pleasure of breast-feeding a baby she would: '*while it was smiling in my face, have plucked my nipple from his boneless gums and dashed the brains out*' (I, vii, 56–58). Finally, when Macbeth is filled with false hope because he has been told by the Second Apparition – appropriately '*a bloody child*' – that '*none of woman born shall harm Macbeth*' (IV, i, 81–82) he is killed by Macduff, who '*was from his mother's womb untimely ripped*' (V, viii, 15–16).

Hospitality

In the feudal Scotland of *Macbeth*, violence is the means by which power is achieved and maintained; but loyalty and a strict social order are what enable the state to function. By killing not only a King, but also a guest within his own house, Macbeth places himself outside the laws of his own society. There are many allusions to social rules and their breakdown, with feasting and banqueting often used as metaphors. To Duncan, Macbeth's valour in battle nourishes the king: '*It is a banquet to me*' (I, iv, 56). But the coronation banquet (III, iv) becomes a scene of terror and an image for the breakdown of order. The murdered Banquo, who should have been the chief guest, returns as a ghost to haunt Macbeth. Lady Macbeth attempts to adhere to the laws of society even after she and her husband have broken them so violently: she needs to uphold the illusion that the social order of her life remains intact. Of Banquo she says: '*If he had been forgotten, it had been as a gap in our great feast, and all thing unbecoming*' (III, i, 11–13). However, on the evening of the banquet, after Macbeth forgets to give the correct toast and begins to speak to Banquo's ghost, she instructs her guests to ignore the rules that hold her society together: '*Stand not upon the order of your going, but go at once*' (III, iv, 119–120). Eating at the Macbeths' table has become an invitation to dine with fear and disorder. '*I have supped full with horrors*' says Macbeth (V, v, 13). For Scotland to return to the correctness of social hospitality, the only solution is for Macbeth to be removed: '*Give to our tables meat, sleep to our nights, free from our feasts and banquets bloody knives*' (III, vi, 34–35).

Glossary of Literary Terms

Act: The major division of a drama; it is usually subdivided into scenes. Like most Classical and Renaissance playwrights, Shakespeare divided his plays into five acts.

Aside: Words spoken by a character in a play which the audience, but not the other characters, can hear. An aside reveals the thoughts and intentions of the character, and may often contrast with what he or she says to the other characters. The first aside in *Macbeth* is in Act I, Scene 3, ll. 115–116, when Macbeth realizes he may indeed become king as the first prophecy has come true. An aside is similar to a soliloquy, except that other characters are present on stage.

Blank verse: Unrhymed verse consisting of five iambic feet (an iamb consists of an unstressed syllable followed by a stressed syllable). It is also called the iambic pentameter. It is often used by Shakespeare as it is close to the rhythmic patterns of English speech. However, blank verse very rarely follows the iambic metre closely.

> *So fóul / and fáir / a dáy / I háve / not séen* (I, ii, 36)

Enjambement (also '**run-on line**'): In a poem or in blank verse, a sentence that runs on from one line to the next without a pause.

> *What cannot you and I perform upon*
> *The unguarded Duncan?* (I, vii, 69–70)

Prose: Prose is all writing that is not in verse. While Shakespeare usually uses verse forms like blank verse, he also employs prose in various scenes in *Macbeth*. The most famous is the Porter scene (Act II, Scene 3). As the porter is obscene and common, prose is more appropriate than verse. Prose is also used by Lady Macbeth when she goes insane (Act V, Scene 1).

Rhyming couplets: Two successive rhyming lines. In *Macbeth* Shakespeare uses rhyming couplets mostly for the witches' spells and dialogues:

When shall we three meet ***again****?*
In thunder, lightening, or in ***rain****?* (I, i, 1–2)

They can also be used to end a soliloquy:

'Hear it not, Duncan, for it is a ***knell***
That summons thee to heaven or to ***hell****.'* (II, i, 63–64)

The couplets often indicate that a decision has been taken or ideas have been summed up.

Scene: A subdivision of an act of a play, usually consisting of unity of time, place and action

Soliloquy: A speech delivered by a character alone on stage. It is used to reveal a character's thoughts, feelings or motives to the audience. It allows the audience to learn more about the character than would be possible if only action and dialogue were presented. In *Macbeth* most of the soliloquies are spoken by Macbeth and show his state of mind as he grapples with his indecision and his weighing up of good and bad. Lady Macbeth is introduced by a soliloquy that immediately makes her both fascinating and repelling.

Stage directions: A playwright's notes in the text of a play which give information about how the drama is to be performed. Stage directions may deal with any of the following: setting, scenery, characters' appearances and manner of speaking, and entrances and exits by characters. We do not know if Shakespeare wrote the stage directions, but certainly in the first published text of *Macbeth* (1623), there are no indications where the action takes place. Later editors have added locations.

Tetrameters: A line consisting of four metres. In Macbeth tetrameters are used by the witches. The tetrameters consist of trochees (a stressed syllable followed by an unstressed syllable). The rhythms give a strong beat to their speech, which sounds far removed from normal speech.

Dóuble, / *dóuble* / *tóil and* / *tróuble* (IV, i, 10)

Coping with Exam Papers

Generally, tasks on texts, whether they are fictional or non-fictional, fall into three categories: 1) **comprehension**, 2) **analysis** and 3) writing a **composition** or a **personal comment**.

1. Comprehension:

All comprehension tasks aim at finding out whether you have **understood** *Macbeth*, regardless of whether you are dealing with an extract or asked to deal with the whole work. Basically, you have to reproduce – in your own words – what is in the text. Usually you are given an extract and are asked to **locate** the passage within the framework of the whole play. Here, select the relevant events which lead up to the passage or which take place afterwards. When answering comprehension questions you should refrain from stating your own opinion, unless you are expressly asked to do so.

2. Analysis:

Analysis tasks go beyond a simple understanding of the text. You may be asked to deal with the whole play or to deal with the selected extract in detail. Analysis questions often concern language and imagery, characters, or the way the plot is structured. Here again, you should avoid giving your own opinion. Be careful not to retell the story: you really need to analyse what is happening on a more abstract level, e.g. don't just say what a character does, but explain why he or she does it, or find an adjective to describe the character, etc.

3. Evaluation

This area covers a wide range of different tasks. Indeed you may be offered a choice of two tasks.

You may be asked to write a composition or a comment, which often require you to show that you have understood what the intention of the play is. Tasks often deal with a general interpretation of *Macbeth*, so make sure your ideas are plausible and well argued. This means that your ideas have to be in line with the play and that you must always be able to prove what you say by referring to the play. Never just make a supposition and leave it at that.

You may be asked to write a 'personal comment', which means you are obliged to give your own opinion, so make sure you base it on informed judgement and avoid making statements which you cannot prove. A thorough knowledge of the play is, of course, the best help you can have.

Often you will be given the choice of doing a 'creative task'. Although at first these may seem easy, you should only choose to do a creative task if you have practised enough beforehand and your teacher seems happy with your work in this area. Creative tasks can involve:

- a change of perspective (i.e. recounting events or situations from the point of view of another character)
- reflection on other characters or events: this can often be in the form of a diary entry
- filling in the gaps: here you might be asked to fill in what the reader does not learn directly from the text. This can often be in the form of a letter, an extra scene or an additional piece of dialogue.

Whatever kind of creative tasks are set, you must remember to stay within the context of *Macbeth*. This means that you should not simply fantasize but should look, for example, at the way a certain character behaves. With *Macbeth* you will obviously not be expected to reproduce the language of Shakespeare, but you should express your ideas in everyday English.

Operative words

Regardless of which category of tasks you are dealing with, it is extremely important to read the task carefully and look for the operative words, which tell you exactly what is required of you. Here is a list of the most common operative words, in alphabetical order. (They are not necessarily confined to either comprehension, analysis or composition)

Analyse …: An analysis is a detailed examination of, for example, a topic central to *Macbeth*, a specific technique used in the play, or one or more of the characters, so you must deal carefully with all the relevant aspects.

Assess …: Here, you must consider in a balanced way the points for and against something.

Comment on …: Here you are allowed to give your personal opinion on, for example, the plot or the way characters behave, but you must always give evidence from the play to support your opinion.

Compare …: You must highlight similarities and differences, most frequently between characters or perhaps different settings within one work. A similar kind of task is:

Contrast …: Here, however, you should concentrate on the differences.

Describe …: In this kind of task you must show what something (e.g. setting) or somebody (one or more of the characters) is like by giving a detailed account. Be careful not to forget any relevant details and choose examples from the play to illustrate the points you have made.

Discuss …: If you are asked to discuss an particular aspect of *Macbeth* (which could be, for example, its themes and topics or the characters and how they interact), you should examine the issue from all sides before you state your personal opinion.

Evaluate …: Here you must form an opinion after carefully considering and presenting the advantages and disadvantages of a particular situation or course of action.

Examine …: This is another way of asking you to **analyse** something.

Explain…: This kind of task often involves giving reasons for the action, characters' motives or how the specific use of certain techniques like the use of imagery produce a certain effect.

Characterize / Describe somebody's character …: Here, you should describe the specific features of, most often, one or more characters, by looking at how they are presented and the way they speak.

Illustrate …: Here, you have to make something clear by choosing relevant examples. Read the task carefully to find out whether you have to concentrate on the given passage or whether you may, or have to, refer to the whole play.

Interpret …: Here, you should deal with both form and content and how they work together to create meaning.

Justify …: Here, you must argue why something should be done or some decision taken or why some conclusion was made.

Outline …: An outline is a general account of something. In other words, an outline can re-tell the major events of the story, or give a brief description of a character, which includes only the very relevant elements only and omits all details.

Point out ...: Here, you must find and explain certain aspects of the play.
Present ...: Here, you are expected to write something down in your words.
State ...: Here, you are expected to specify clearly whatever is required. You may be required to state the main features or development of something.
Summarize ...: A summary is more precise than an outline. When writing a summary you should select the key points and ideas, etc. and structure them. As in an outline you should not go into detail or give examples. You might, for example, be asked to summarize a soliloquy, or the events of the whole play or an extract.

General points to remember – or how to impress the examiner:

- You are not writing for yourself, but you are addressing the examiner(s) who will mark your work. Examiners are not mind-readers, so you must express yourself as clearly as possible.
- Always collect and organize your ideas before you start writing. This will allow the examiner to be able to follow you more easily.
- When writing a composition or a personal comment, remember three simple steps: say what you are going to say – say it – say what you have said. Doing this will make your text more convincing.
- When you are dealing with literature you should always use the simple present tense when discussing characters and action.
- Structure your work by using so-called 'connectives' to link your ideas, so that the examiner can follow the presentation of your arguments. Otherwise he or she may get the impression that you are 'rambling'. You should be able to find a list of connectives in your coursebook.
- Likewise, avoid all forms of repetition, unless you want to return to a point you made earlier on. In this case you should use expressions like 'as I have already pointed out ...'.
- You can always impress the examiner by using suitable quotes, but they should only be used to **underline** a point you have already made or are going to make, and not instead of making a point – otherwise the examiner will think you are simply copying from the text or that you are unable to express yourself correctly. Always put

your quotations in inverted commas. If you are allowed to use the book, you should also refer to the page and line of the quote. When quoting from *Macbeth*, you should ask your teacher how he or she would like you to quote. In this book the quotes are given as if they were prose; this was done to emphasize the content. The normal way of quoting Shakespeare's plays is as follows: 'Tomorrow, and tomorrow, and tomorrow / Creeps in this petty pace from day to day / To the last syllable of recorded time' (V, v, 18–20). Each line of verse is separated by a slash (/) and the new line begins with a capital letter. Should you be quoting prose sentences, you should quote as you would from a novel, etc.: 'Out damned spot! Out I say! – One, two; why, then, 'tis time to do't. – Hell is murky. – Fie, my lord, fie!' (V, I, 33–34)

- Usually the test paper will tell you how many words you have to write for each section of the test. If you have time after re-reading and checking your paper for coherence, mistakes, etc., try and count your words, as you may have marks deducted for writing too little or too much.

Written Test

At some stage while reading Macbeth in class, you will have to do a written test. What the test looks like depends on how much of the play you have read, and to a certain extent on the *Bundesland* you are in. Here you are offered two written tests.

A Soliloquy

Is this a dagger which I see before me,
The handle toward my hand? Come, let me clutch thee.
I have thee not, and yet I see thee still.
Art thou not, fatal vision, sensible
To feeling as to sight? Or art thou but
A dagger of the mind, a false creation,
Proceeding from the heat-oppressèd brain?
I see thee yet, in form as palpable
As this which now I draw.
Thou marshall'st me the way that I was going,
And such an instrument I was to use.
Mine eyes are made the fools o' the other senses,
Or else worth all the rest. I see thee still,
And on thy blade and dudgeon gouts of blood,
Which was not so before. There's no such thing:
It is the bloody business which informs
Thus to mine eyes. Now o'er the one half-world
Nature seems dead, and wicked dreams abuse
The curtained sleep. Witchcraft celebrates
Pale Hecate's offerings, and withered Murder,
Alarum'd by his sentinel, the wolf,
Whose howl's his watch, thus with his stealthy pace,
With Tarquin's ravishing strides, towards his design
Moves like a ghost. Thou sure and firm-set earth,
Hear not my steps, which way they walk, for fear
Thy very stones prate of my whereabout,
And take the present horror from the time,
Which now suits with it. Whiles I threat, he lives:

Words to the heat of deeds too cold breath gives.
[*A bell rings.*]
I go, and it is done. The bell invites me.
Hear it not, Duncan, for it is a knell
That summons thee to heaven or to hell.
[*Exit.*]

39 **heat-oppressèd**: feverish

40 **palpable**: touchable

42 **thou marshall'st me**: you lead me

46 **dudgeon**: handle

46 **gouts**: drops

52 **Hecate**: goddess of witchcraft

53 **sentinel**: watchman

54 **watch**: way of telling the time at night

55 **Tarquin**: a Roman king who raped and mutilated his friend's wife, Lucrece. To Shakespeare's audience, he was a symbol of betrayal and cruelty.

55 **design**: purpose, fulfilment of his plans

58 **prate**: tell, talk

60 **suits with**: is right for

60 **threat**: threaten

64 **knell**: funeral bell

Tasks:

1 **Briefly explain the situation Macbeth is in when he speaks this soliloquy, and say what it is about.**

2 **Analyse the soliloquy with special focus on how it tells you about Macbeth's state of mind (e.g. through the structure, images, etc.). What do you think the soliloquy should sound like? (Choose two or more lines to which you might add stage directions for the actor.)**

3 **Imagine you were in the audience watching *Macbeth*. What emotions would this soliloquy evoke in you with regard to your assessment of the character Macbeth so far? (Remember how you first encountered Macbeth, and what steps you have seen him take with regard to the murder he is about to commit.)**

Either

a) Write a comment.

Or

b) Invent a dialogue in the interval in which you talk to a friend specifically about this soliloquy.

Dealing with the test

This soliloquy is one of the best-known from Macbeth, so it would be quite wise to get to know it in detail anyway. What is written below are not answers, but hints and things for you to think about so that you can write your own answer.

1

Most of Macbeth's inner conflict occurs before the murder of Duncan, so this soliloquy can be placed before the murder. After the murder, Macbeth finds murdering more mechanical, but he still suffers from pangs of guilt (e.g. his sighting of Banquo's ghost at the banquet.)

As this is a soliloquy, one can imagine that Macbeth is expressing his true thoughts.

Here the audience is shown how Macbeth is not a steadfast character who acts without a conscience. Indeed we see how disturbed he is by the act of murder he is about to commit.

Writing your answer

When you write your answer, you need to give a convincing opening sentence that relates to the question. Something along these lines: 'This soliloquy takes place at the beginning of Act II just before Macbeth murders Duncan.'

You are asked to 'explain the situation Macbeth is in'. Here you need to mention what has happened before: that the witches have prophesized that he will become king, that Duncan has named Malcolm as his successor, which makes Macbeth's ambition to be king more difficult to achieve, that Lady Macbeth is very keen to have Duncan murdered and her husband made king, and that she has persuaded him through a mixture of insults and love to commit murder, that Macbeth himself is still not convinced that he can kill Duncan.

You are also asked to explain what the soliloquy 'is about'. Here you need to say that Macbeth is undergoing internal conflict which is reflected in his vision of a bloody dagger, which seems to lead him in the direction of the room where Duncan is sleeping, and that he finally overcomes his doubts and accepts the need to kill Duncan in order to become king, but that he has also accepted the image of darkness and murder that he will soon embody.

When answering this question, you should avoid quoting and listing any images, etc. from the soliloquy. This answer should be written in your own words.

2

The structure reflects the change from Macbeth's rational state of mind to mental disturbance. Three times Macbeth repeats the words 'I see thee', then tries to question his vision, by asking whether this dagger should not be 'sensible to feeling', 'palpable'. He is in a unusual state of seeing something but knowing that it cannot exist. He appeals to the world of the senses ('sensible', 'mine eyes are made the fool of the other senses', 'informs thus to mine eyes'). This why Macbeth is such a fascinating character: he acts but questions his actions, he sees but questions his sight.

The soliloquy changes in l.47 when Macbeth dismisses the vision understanding that 'it is the bloody business which informs thus to mine eyes'. Until then he was questioning, now he knows it is his mind that is playing tricks on him.

The main symbol is obviously the dagger. It is the symbol of the action Macbeth needs to take if he is to achieve his ambition and become king. It becomes covered in blood, another symbol that occurs throughout the play.

Once he has overcome his fears, his images are taken from the world of evil and death: 'nature seems dead', 'wicked dreams', 'witchcraft', 'pale Hecate', 'withered murder', 'wolf', 'Tarquin'. This accumulation of unpleasant images would have had a strong effect on the audience of the time which was more prone to these forms of superstition. Macbeth, as always, initially uncertain, resolves to carry through with the murder and sees himself as the personification of murder. Yet he is aware of the terribleness of his crime and asks for the earth not to reveal his steps. There is an element of fatality, of not wishing to be involved ('I go, and it is done'), which reflects Lady Macbeth's words: 'what thou wouldst highly, that wouldst thou holily' (I, v, 19–20), i.e. Macbeth does not really like getting his hands dirty.

Finally a bell rings, his signal to act, but it is also a symbol representing the call to death for Duncan.

How you think the soliloquy should sound will be an individual decision, but certainly the actor should express fear as well as strength. His fear reflects the fact that he does not want to commit murder, the strength will reflect the fact he must overcome his doubts. So the first part (up to l. 47) will express more doubts, while after that he must sound as though he is trying to convince himself of what he is doing.

There are a few occasions where an extra stage direction would be useful, e.g. l. 40: [*Macbeth draws his sword.*] Otherwise the decisions are yours. One possibility for l. 39 might be: [*Macbeth puts his hands to his head and crumples up on the floor as if in pain.*]

Writing your answer

Remember that here 'analysis' is required, so avoid rewriting what is said in the soliloquy. Style is always an important factor in analysing how an author achieves a particular effect. For this you will need vocabulary such as 'images', 'metaphors', 'metaphorical language'; words reflecting the state of Macbeth's mind like 'anxious', 'uncertain', 'worried', 'brave', 'reproachful', 'hesitant' and 'determined' may be useful. Furthermore you will need to use the words that cover the particular areas that Macbeth discusses: 'murder', 'regicide', 'evil', 'crime'.

Your task is to link all these ideas together. You will find words and phrases like 'show', 'illustrate', 'demonstrate', 'seem', 'appear to be', 'probably' and 'possibly' will help.

Connectives (e.g. 'moreover','on the one hand … on the other …') will also come in useful for making your text coherent.

An example might be: 'The dagger which Macbeth sees does not seem to be real. It is most likely a figment of his imagination, yet nevertheless it reflects his uncertain state of mind. It is a powerful image preparing the audience for the murder that will soon be committed.'

When discussing how the soliloquy should sound, it is important to refer to the formal structure of the soliloquy. Here phrases like 'blank verse' and 'rhyming couplets' (cf. pp. 79 and 80) will come in handy, while you will need other words like 'pause', 'low voice', 'high-pitched voice', 'shout out' and 'trembling voice' when you state how you believe the soliloquy should be delivered.

3

Naturally, if you have been fortunate enough to see a performance of *Macbeth*, you are at an advantage, as you can use the emotions you felt at the time. Nevertheless, the question is not really asking you to think of the stage version but to express your feelings at this speech in general. Possible things to consider might be: Macbeth's inner conflict, his mental disturbance, his apparent attempt to escape responsibility, his fatalistic approach to his forthcoming action, his tendency to think too much about his actions.

Writing your answer

Your answer should be based very much on what you analysed in task 2, so avoid writing anything that contradicts what you wrote earlier. Your style should be neutral if you are writing a comment. If you are writing the dialogue, you should situate the dialogue in the opening sentences, e.g. 'So, what did you think of the actor's delivery of the soliloquy "Is this a dagger ...?"'. The dialogue partners must react to the other's statements. The style should remain informal but should avoid slang (they are at a performance of *Macbeth*!).

Really Good Quotes

Below are some quotes that you should try to remember, as they are well-known.

FIRST WITCH: *When shall we three meet again?*
In thunder, lightning, or in rain?
SECOND WITCH: *When the hurlyburly's done,*
When the battle's lost, and won.
(I, i, 1–4)

Fair is foul, and foul is fair.
(I, i, 12)

So foul and fair a day I have not seen.
(I, iii, 36)

the seeds of time
(I, iii, 56)

Nothing in his life
Became him like the leaving it.
(I, iv, 7–8)

To throw away the dearest thing he owed,
As 'twere a careless trifle.
(I, iv, 10–11)

the milk of human kindness
(I, v, 16)

Come, you spirits [...] unsex me here, [...] make thick my blood
(I, v, 39–42)

Look like the innocent flower,
But be the serpent under't.
(I, v, 64–65)

Is this a dagger which I see before me,
The handle toward my hand?
(II, i, 33–34)

Methought I heard a voice cry, 'Sleep no more!
Macbeth does murder sleep.'
(II, ii, 34–35)

Will all great Neptune's ocean wash this blood
Clean from my hand?
(II, ii, 59–60)

Lechery, sir, it [drinking] provokes, and unprovokes; it provokes the desire, but it takes away the performance.
(II, iii, 27–29)

To be thus is nothing,
But to be safely thus.
(III, i, 49–50)

Double, double toil and trouble;
Fire burn, and cauldron bubble.
(IV, i, 10–11)

By the pricking of my thumbs,
Something wicked this way comes.
(IV, i, 44–45)

None of woman born
Shall harm Macbeth.
(IV, i, 81–82)

Out, damned spot! Out, I say!
(V, i, 33)

Yet who would have thought the old man to have had so much blood in him.
(V, i, 36–38)

Here's the smell of the blood still; all the perfumes of Arabia will not sweeten this little hand.
(V, i, 47–48)

What's done cannot be undone.
(V, i, 62–63)

Tomorrow, and tomorrow, and tomorrow
Creeps in this pretty pace from day to day
To the last syllable of recorded time;
And all our yesterdays have lighted fools
The way to dusty death. Out, out, brief candle!
Life's but a walking shadow, a poor player
That struts and frets his hour upon the stage
And then is heard no more. It is a tale
Told by an idiot, full of sound and fury
Signifying nothing.
(V, v, 18–27)